Fifty Hikes
in Central
Pennsylvania

West Branch of the Susquehanna from Hyner View

FIFTY HIKES IN CENTRAL PENN- SYLVANIA

Walks, Day Hikes, and Backpacking Trips in the Keystone State

TOM THWAITES

Photographs by the Author

 New Hampshire Publishing Company
Somersworth

Acknowledgments

Many of the hikes in this book were suggested either by members of the Keystone Trails Association or by employees of the Pennsylvania Department of Environmental Resources, particularly those in the Bureau of Forestry. I would like to thank all those members of Keystone Trails Association and its member organizations who build and maintain hiking trails in Penn's Woods.

I am grateful to Dave Raphael, Charles Salkins, Maury Forrester, Rob Carey, and all the other companions who hiked with me in the course of this book. I am particularly grateful to my wife, Barbara, who served both as hiking companion and typist.

I would also like to thank my editor, Donna McEachern, for her help and encouragement.

An Invitation to the Reader

If you find that conditions have changed along these trails, please let the author and publisher know so that corrections may be made in future editions. Address all correspondence:

Editor, 50 Hikes
New Hampshire Publishing Company
Somersworth, NH 03878

International Standard Book Number: 0-89725-002-8
Library of Congress Catalog Card Number: 78-71141
© 1979 by Thomas T. Thwaites
All rights reserved
Published by New Hampshire Publishing Company
Somersworth, New Hampshire
Printed in the United States of America
Photograph on page 139 by Rebecca Thwaites
Design by Wladislaw Finne

*To the memory of
my niece, Laura Braun*

Contents

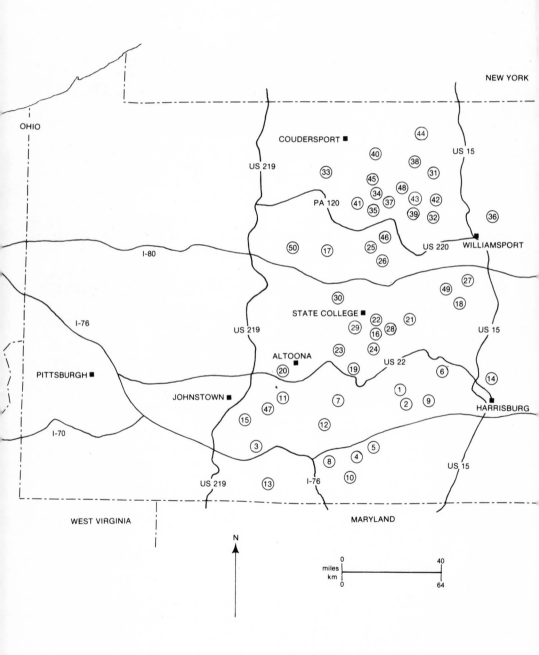

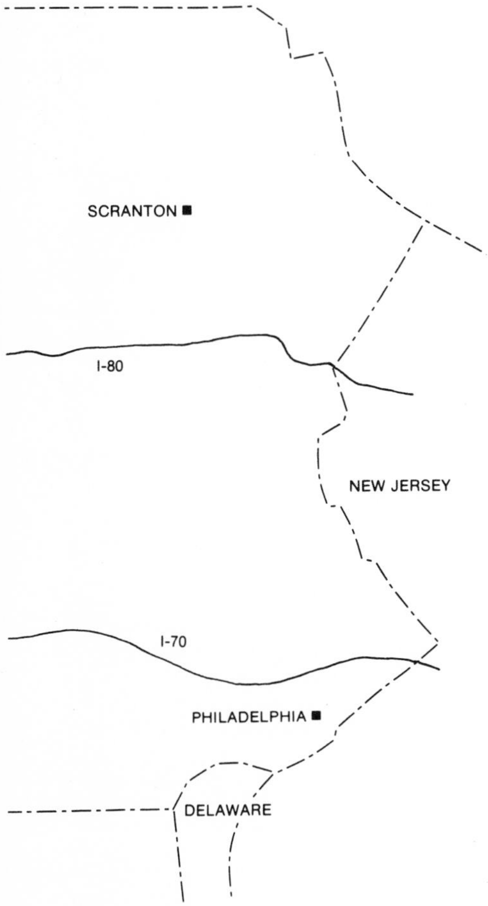

SCRANTON ■

I-80

NEW JERSEY

I-70

PHILADELPHIA ■

DELAWARE

Introduction   9

South District

Middle District

North District

Backpacking Trips

Introduction

Along one of the many old logging railroad grades

Between the heavily used Appalachian Trail in Pennsylvania's southeast and the widely known Allegheny National Forest in its opposite corner lies a broad but often ignored expanse of Penn's Woods with some of the best hiking in the Northeast.

Here, in Central Pennsylvania, little-used trails take you along ridges, through valleys, and across plateaus. The views from this region's endless mountains are pleasing and varied, even though none of the peaks aspires to timber line, let alone a snow cap. On one side of a ridge prosperous farms may checker the valley, and on the other the waves of the forest sea roll unbroken to the horizon. While other trails in Pennsylvania are being loved to death by increasing numbers of hikers, many trails in this area are slowly disappearing under the relentless growth of huckleberries, mountain laurel, and scrub oak.

The total length of these central Pennsylvania trails, which are mostly on public land, is estimated to exceed that of the Appalachian and Pacific Crest trails together. For a region surrounded on three sides by urbanized areas, this is a remarkable resource. A system of wild and natural areas totaling 165,000 acres has been established within Pennsylvania's state forests. This book contains twenty-one of these areas, as well as two not yet in the system.

The Penn's Woods described in this book is long on silence, solitude, and history. Pennsylvania probably has more ghost towns than Colorado, but since wood doesn't last here as it does in the desert mountains of the West, they are not as visible or dramatic. Old roads, railroad grades, and log slides lie along many hikes, remnants of a once populous and productive era.

If you are a hiker, I urge you to switch from overused trails elsewhere to the underused trails in Penn's Woods. If you are not hiking yet, I hope to convince you the only way to see and experience Penn's Woods is to get out of your car and back on your feet. When you have the hiking habit try backpacking—you will be free to roam Penn's Woods with a maximum of independence.

Trails

These hikes include a variety of trails. Some are blazed and maintained on a regular basis; others are merely identified by signs at intersections and depend on use to remain clear. The system of blazed trails on public lands is expanding rapidly, and every year new ones are added and old ones extended or relocated. Many relocations reduce road walking or permit a more scenic, historic, or pleasing route. (These relocations, of course, may cause a section of a trail to differ from its description here.)

Footwear

Through-hikers on the Appalachian Trail invariably report that Pennsylvania has the rockiest part of the 2,000-mile-long route. Proper hiking boots are a must for most of these hikes. I recommend medium-weight boots, six inches high, with lugged soles and waterproofing. When you buy boots be sure to fit them over the socks you wear hiking—a thin, inner pair and a thick, mostly wool, outer pair. Some hikes are identified in the text as negotiable with rubber-soled walking shoes. Children get by with sneakers on such trails but adults wearing sneakers invite sprained ankles.

Clothing and Equipment

On summer hikes the task is keeping cool, so shorts and short-sleeved shirts are best. Remember that cotton will keep you cooler than synthetics. Most people forget a day pack.
In a frameless day pack you should carry no more than ten to eleven pounds of gear, which should include the following:

1. Water. Although you can drink from most springs and many streams in Penn's Woods, the available sources dry up at times and not every hike has water.
2. Food. You should include a meat bar, bag of gorp, tin of pemmican, or other emergency food, as well as your lunch.
3. Rain parka or poncho. Rain is inevitable in Pennsylvania. Be ready for it.
4. Windbreaker, or wool shirt or sweater. You should always be prepared for cold. A Gore-Tex rain parka can double.
5. Pocket knife with can opener.
6. Small first-aid kit with bandages, moleskin, aspirin, and first-aid cream.
7. Flashlight. Hiking a trail in the dark is no fun, and darkness comes early on a cloudy November day.
8. Map and compass. These are optional on most hikes but may prove reassuring on some, such as Splash Dam Hollow.
9. Miscellaneous. Insect repellent (seasonal); toilet paper (always); identification guides to birds, trees or wildflowers; extra roll of film; and spare spectacles all come in handy. In addition, a brimmed hat keeps the sun off ears and neck, reduces areas vulnerable to insect attack, and keeps rain off glasses.

Hiking during spring and fall is more enjoyable than in summer. The insects are gone, it's cooler, and you find wildflowers or colored leaves along the trail. In these seasons wool shows its miraculous qualities. Long pants and a long-sleeved shirt of light wool keep you comfortable even in bad weather. Again, you want extra clothing in your pack in case of rain or real cold.

Winter hiking calls for a shirt and pants of heavier wool. You will be surprised at how warm you can be on winter hikes—as long as you keep moving. However, you need a parka or sweater when stationary. A sitting pad of quarter-inch ensolite is welcome if you rest amid snow and ice. And winter is no time to leave your canteen behind. The dry air leaves you thirsty.

Don't forget gaiters to close the gap between boot tops and pant cuffs.

Backpacking

A real treat in Penn's Woods is back-packing on state forest lands. A camp-site reservation is unnecessary and sites are still available at noon. It's like backpacking was in New England or the Adirondacks fifty years ago, and you're likely to have a site to yourself with the illusion you are the first to be there. Be aware that the five hikes designated herein for backpacking are lengthy trips. For your first back-packing experience select a day hike with an overnight option (see Hikes 8, 9, 12, 13, 15, 25, 28, 36, 37, 38, 39, 40, 43, and 45).

You need a frame pack with a *padded hipbelt*, a good sleeping bag, and a tent or tarp—there are no shelters on these trails. The padded hipbelt, a revolution in backpacks, transfers the weight of your pack from your shoulders to your hips, thus by-passing your back. Packs, bags, and tents are big ticket items but it's usually possible to rent them if you're not ready to buy. (The number of manufacturers and designs can be bewildering. *Backpacker Magazine* rates them in the most comprehensive list I have seen.)

Here are a few tips on sleeping bags. First, your best bet is a mummy bag. It is warmer than a rectangular bag of the same weight. Some are confining but others are cut gener-ously and you should find a style that suits. Second, do not feel you must have now-expensive down items. Down gear is certainly necessary in the dry, desert mountains of the west, where almost all precipitation comes as snow and the cold and stormy weather warrants extra protection. In Pennsylvania's climate you can wear outer garments that are less expensive and still provide warmth. Down also has two related drawbacks—when wet it ceases to insulate, and it is impos-sible to dry in the field. Look for Polar-guard and Holofill II; they insulate when wet and are relatively easy to dry, so are better suited to the tem-perate rain forests of Appalachia.

For cooking, small backpacking stoves are superior to the old-fashioned campfire. They are a minimal fire hazard, don't leave soot on your pots, and don't deplete the firewood supply. Furthermore, they heat food in a fraction of the time it takes to find firewood, cut it, and begin the fire, and they function in wet weather.

There's no need to use expensive, freeze-dried food for a weekend or three-day backpacking trip. Get super-market dried foods and mixes, such as soups, tuna, hamburger and other helpers, along with oatmeal, cheese, and concentrated foods. Small cans of tuna, ham, or other meat are suitable but remember to carry out empty cans after washing them to prevent your pack from smelling. Also, opaque foils contain a layer of unburnable alumi-num and must be carried out.

For a week-long trip you definitely

One of the new biunitary signs

need some freeze-dried or dehydrated food to keep pack weight down to twenty-five percent of body weight. An alternative may be a food drop or cache halfway along the route.

Before your first trip set up the tent in your own yard to make sure you have all its parts. Make sure the stove works properly too. Boil some water and compare the time it takes to the stated value for your model.

Safety in the Woods

Compared to the risk of an auto accident driving to and from the trailhead, the woods are very safe. Pennsylvania has an estimated 1,500 extremely shy bears, and while you may see signs of bear, your chance of encountering one is slim.

Copperheads and timber rattlers can appear on any trail, and it pays to watch your step on warm days. Although it's extremely rare for a hiker to be bitten, it is a good idea to know the warning buzz of a timber rattler, as it tells you of unseen snakes. The cut-and-suck snake bite kits usually do more harm than good, at least in untrained hands. In the event of a snake bite, the victim should be carried to a hospital for administration of anti-venom. If possible, the snake body should also be taken for identification. The snake may turn out to be nonpoisonous.

Lightning is a real hazard to hikers, as ridges are frequently hit. If you are

The Beech Bottom Trail

caught on a ridge in a thunderstorm, move down the side to a uniformly high stand of trees.

Don't hike during bear or deer hunting seasons in late November and early December. However, hunting is prohibited on Sundays, and if you've just got to get out on the trails, hike then.

About This Book

The fifty hikes in this book were selected for their wide range of hiking experiences and to introduce hikers to Pennsylvania's wild and natural areas as well as its organized trails. They range from walks that take less than an hour to a week-long backpacking trip. I have made every effort to devise circuit hikes, and those that cannot be looped are included as short out-and-back hikes or longer car shuttle hikes. All of one hike, Blair Trail, and parts of the Kettle Creek Vista, Owl Hollow and Summerson Run, and the Lost Turkey hikes cross private land. However, these are blazed and maintained trails, and land owners have given permission for trail use by the public. I hope hikers' conduct allows this happy situation to continue.

The hikes are uniformly distributed over three areas in the central portion of the state. The south district runs from the Mason-Dixon Line north to US 22. The central district extends from there north to PA 120 and US 220. The north district stretches from that line to the New York border. Each district has five introductory, or half-day, hikes and ten day hikes. Within each district hikes have been ordered according to total distance, which is closely related to overall difficulty. The dividing line between an introductory and a day hike is three hours or 5 miles (8 km). Backpacking trips require two or more days.

The summary headings for each hike listing total distance, walking time, and vertical rise should help you decide which hikes match your capabilities and the time you have available.

Total distance is the distance walked when you complete the described route. Most hikes can be shortened and some include directions for specific shortcuts. This book gives hiking distances in both traditional and metric units. Pennsylvania trails are in process of converting to metric measure. Current editions of guidebooks for the Appalachian Trail in Pennsylvania, and the Tuscarora, Mid State and Black Forest trails use both sets of units, some trails already have biunitary distance signs, and one trail, Lost Turkey, is equipped with kilometer posts. Each hike in this book, with the exception of the Golden Eagle Trail, was measured with a Model 660 M measuring wheel manufactured by the Rolatape Corporation of Los Angeles. Distances measured with a wheel are more reliable than those done with a pedometer. Driving directions to the trailheads are given in miles only, however.

Walking times are set for a middle-aged pace and do not take into account extended lunch stops or other breaks. Novice hikers probably won't match these times but, with experience, the young can no doubt surpass them.

Vertical rise is the total amount of climbing along the route. It may occur all in one climb, in which case it is the difference between the lowest and highest points on the route. But it may and frequently does occur over several climbs. If there are any descents between these climbs then the vertical rise noted for the hike will *exceed* the difference between the lowest and highest points on the hike. Vertical rise, which is listed in feet and meters, can turn even the shortest hike into a real challenge. A sketch map showing the route and key landmarks is included with each hike.

If you find yourself becoming an avid hiker, I recommend you join a hiking club. You can find the nearest one through Keystone Trails Association. A hiking club allows you to meet others similarly enthused—and to help maintain the trails in Penn's Woods. It is a well-kept secret that maintaining a hiking trail is one of the most satisfying outdoor activities known.

Happy Hiking!

Other Helpful Information

Pennsylvania Hiking Trails. 8th edition 1978. Published by Keystone Trails Association. Available from

Preparing a log bridge

Appalachian Trail Conference, P.O.
Box 236, Harper's Ferry, WV 25425.

Hiking Guide to Western Pennsylvania. 4th edition 1978. Published by
Pittsburgh Council, American Youth
Hostels, Inc., 6300 Fifth Avenue, Pittsburgh, PA 15232. Despite its name this
guide also covers Central Pennsylvania.

*Hiking Trails in the Mid Atlantic
States.* By Edward B. Garvey. Published by Great Lakes Living Press,
Matteson, IL 1976.

Foot trail information on U.S. Geological Survey topographical maps is
the least reliable information and the
quality of such information is highly
variable from one map to the next.
Topographical maps are available from
the U.S. Geological Survey, 1200
South Eads St., Arlington, VA 22202,
and in most backpacking stores.

For a copy of the official Pennsylvania Transportation Map showing
most organized hiking trails as well as
state forest, game lands, and parks,
write to: Travel Development Bureau,
Pennsylvania Department of Commerce, Harrisburg, PA 17120.

The umbrella hiking organization in
Penn's Woods is the Keystone Trails
Association, R.D. 3, Box 261, Cogan
Station, PA 17728. Membership, as of
this writing, is still only two dollars a
year.

South District

1 Path Valley Railroad Tunnel

Total distance: 1.3 miles (2.1 km)
Walking time: ¾ hour
Vertical rise: 300 feet (90 meters)

On this short hike you visit the ruins of two narrow-gauge railroads. The ruins, in the vicinity of Big Spring State Park in Tuscarora State Forest, are all that remain of the hope and determination of railroad officials and the hard work of laborers at the turn of the century.

The first remnant is an incomplete railroad tunnel intended to carry the Path Valley Railroad through Conocheague Mountain into Path Valley. In 1893 the Path Valley Railroad was chartered and began construction of the grade and the tunnel that was to be a half mile (800 meters) long. With great confidence in its surveyors, the company started construction from both sides of the mountain. The mountainside was covered with a deep layer of loose and broken rock on the west, or Path Valley, side. Digging never reached the solid rock to form a tunnel entrance.

On the east side, which you visit, workers hit hard rock immediately. The forces that produced these folded mountains hundreds of millions of years ago also metamorphosed the rock into flint. The flint resisted blasting and progress was slow. Initial efforts to dig the tunnel ended in 1895 when unpaid workmen abandoned the project. In 1910 a final effort was made to complete it but the total distance tunneled was only 37 meters.

In comparison, the Perry Lumber Company's railroad, whose grade you also travel, was a success. The company purchased a single Climax loco-

motive, acquired 19,000 acres of western Perry County, and in the space of four years (1901-1905) cut the entire tract. The company appears to have been relatively efficient. According to authorities on Pennsylvania logging, many other operations left bark and hardwood to rot on the hillsides, but Perry sold the bark to tanneries and used the leftover hardwood for barrel staves and chemical wood. The company's lands were eventually purchased by the state and became part of the present Tuscarora State Forest.

To reach Big Spring State Park drive 5.8 miles southwest from New Germantown on PA 274, or 4.8 miles northeast from the junction of PA 274 and PA 75 near Doylesburg. Turn off PA 274 at Hemlock Road, which is just west of the main parking area for the state park. Cross a culvert and bear left into a small parking area. The hike, for which walking shoes are sufficient, begins by the display case containing information on the railroads and the trail.

The blue-blazed trail quickly climbs to the rough end of a Path Valley Railroad grade. The railroad may have intended to use geared locomotives, as the average grade from New Germantown to the tunnel entrance was to be 3.7 percent. Rod-type steam locomotives would have had considerable difficulty on this grade. As you proceed the grade becomes more finished and then ends abruptly. You then descend a set of steps and bear right uphill. As you look ahead you see the end of another grade (the gap between

Old railroad grade

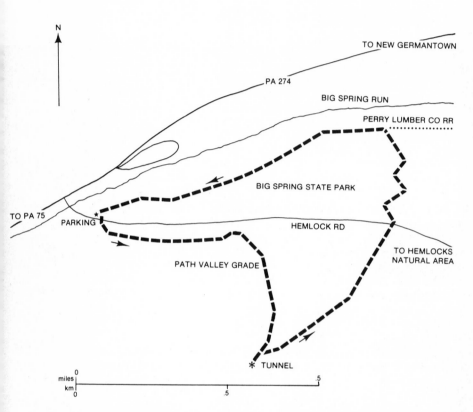

N

TO NEW GERMANTOWN

PA 274

BIG SPRING RUN

PERRY LUMBER CO RR

BIG SPRING STATE PARK

TO PA 75

PARKING

HEMLOCK RD

TO HEMLOCKS
NATURAL AREA

PATH VALLEY GRADE

* TUNNEL

0
miles
km
0   .5

.5

these two was to be filled with rock blasted from the tunnel) and on climbing you find it cuts into the mountainside. The cut is partially filled with fallen rocks and trees have grown among them.

The tunnel opening, barely visible over the rocks, reveals relatively little rockfall inside, but beware of exploring it as the footing is wet and slippery. In wet weather the tunnel may fill with water dammed by the fallen rocks outside.

You continue by following the trail down off the fill at the end of the cut,

crossing Hemlock Road, and then winding downhill to the old Perry Lumber Company railroad grade. To the right the grade heads down the valley to New Germantown, but the trail turns left and leads to the track's end. The company operated a sawmill at this railhead but little evidence of it exists.

You soon reenter Big Spring State Park and bear left around a massive picnic shelter built by the Civilian Conservation Corps in the 1930s. Follow the trail around the main part of the park and head back to the small parking area and your car.

2 Hemlocks Natural Area

Total distance: 1.7 miles (2.7 km)
Walking time: 1 hour
Vertical rise: 400 feet (120 meters)

Tall trees in the natural area

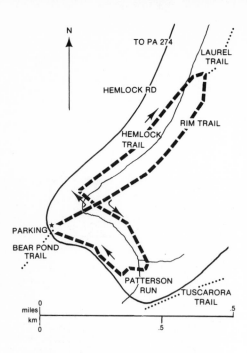

A 120-acre stand of old growth hemlock along Patterson Run in Tuscarora State Forest distinguishes this hike. The trees in this stand are estimated to be three to five hundred years old, and we can only speculate on their survival in the midst of logging country. The brittle hemlock generally brings a low price, and these particular trees are in a steep canyon between Hemlock Mountain and Little Round Top. The trees' low marketability and the difficulty in felling, stripping, and removing them may have influenced the Perry Lumber Company to bypass them during their operations here from 1901–1905.

The hemlocks here approach the maximum size for the species—around 130 feet high and 72 inches in diameter. The tallest tree measured here is 123 feet high and the thickest is 51 inches in diameter. This area has had a special significance since 1931, when the hemlock was designated Pennsylvania's state tree.

To reach the Hemlocks Natural Area drive 5.8 miles southwest from New Germantown on PA 274, or 4.8 miles northeast from the junction of PA 274 and PA 75 near Doylesburg. Turn off PA 274 onto Hemlock Road and drive for 4 miles to a small parking lot across from the Bear Pond Trail. (Along the last 1.5 miles you can see some of the large trees of the natural area.)

Several hiking routes go through the area but the one you take requires a minimum amount of road walking and no backtracking. Walking shoes are adequate although the trail is rocky in places. From the parking lot you follow the wood-chipped path downhill just under 150 yards (130 meters) to a bridge over Patterson Run. Turn left at the junction just across the bridge, and recross Patterson Run on another bridge. The Hemlock Trail becomes rough and rocky as it goes downstream. Bear right at any forks, following this trail across Patterson Run again and up to a junction with the Rim and Laurel trails at .7 mile (1.1 km). Turn sharply right onto the Rim Trail; there are some fine views of the hemlocks farther up the slope.

The Rim Trail leads you back to the junction at the first bridge you crossed; you could truncate your hike now by taking the wood-chipped path back to your car. On this hike, however, turn left, heading upstream on the Hemlock Trail, which crosses the run twice more on bridges before moving up to Hemlock Road. Here you take a right turn and walk .2 mile (400 meters) back to your car. To avoid part of the road walk, bear right when you see the old road; it rejoins the present one at the parking lot.

3 Shawnee State Park

Total distance: 3.5 miles (5.6 km)
Walking time: 1¾ hours
Vertical rise: none

Shadbush in bloom

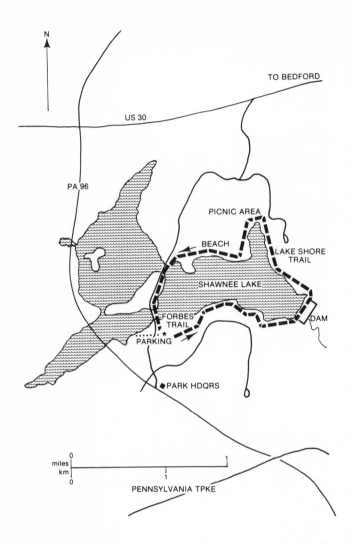

Shawnee State Park, between US 30 and the Pennsylvania Turnpike, surrounds a flood-control reservoir on Shawnee Creek. Despite the intense development of this park, a considerable amount of wildlife flourishes here. As you round the trail into a secluded cove you may see a basking turtle plop off his log, a fishing heron take wing, or a deer bound away. And in a muddy place, the print of a miniature hand may betray the passage of a raccoon. Trees along the trail are pre- dominantly red and white oak, Virginia pine, and hickory. Some of the white oaks appear to be quite old.

This short, easy hike moves around the east portion of Shawnee Lake. The trail is paved in one section and graded most of the way, so shoes or sneakers are adequate. Stay on the path to avoid the many poison ivy patches along the way.

To reach the park entrance drive west from Bedford, the nearest turn- pike exchange, on US 30 for 9 miles.

You begin your hike at Picnic Area 1 on the left-hand side of the main park road, just beyond the second bridge over Shawnee Lake.

The first section follows the Forbes Trail, a remnant of the wagon road cut in 1758 by General John Forbes to take Fort Duquesne in the French and Indian War. After .3 mile (500 meters), the old Forbes Road vanishes into the lake and you bear right on the broad, graded trail, from which you see Shawnee Lake and the Allegheny Front.

In .6 mile (1 km) you bear left on a jeep road and shortly reach the crest of a dam. Proceed across it, bear left at the spillway's edge, and ascend to another roadway. At normal lake level the spillway is well above water, but at flood stage it would be folly to attempt a crossing. For a dam to be of any use in controlling a flood its level must be well below the level at which it would overflow. Ideally the reservoir behind it should be kept empty, but then its recreational value would be negligible.

You now bear left a bit more than 100 yards (100 meters) on the road at the spillway's far edge, and then left again on the Lake Shore Trail. About .4 mile (600 meters) farther the trail skirts a picnic area. (The hike could also be started from this and other areas farther along.) You pass a succession of picnic areas and in .7 mile (1.2 km) reach the beach area, through which the trail is paved. At the top of a rise at the beach area's far end, turn left onto a jeep track, and at the end of that, right over another rise. This shortcut leads to the marina, where many kinds of watercraft can be rented.

At the far side of the marina you reach the main park road. Cross the bridge to the island. Large numbers of barn swallows nest under the bridge and you can see them catch insects on the wing. To the east are Buffalo and Wills mountains.

Continue across the island, to the second bridge and then back to your car. If you would like to extend your walk, a rough section of the Forbes Trail is across the paved road from where you began. After about .3 mile (500 meters), this stretch also vanishes into the lake.

4 Cowans Gap State Park

Total distance: 3.7 miles (5.9 km)
Walking time: 2¼ hours
Vertical rise: 600 feet (180 meters)

Cowans Gap, a wind gap through Tuscarora Mountain, is located in Buchanan State Forest. A wind gap is formed when a stream that originally flowed across the grain of the ridge and valley region is captured by a stream that flows with the grain. This happens because the latter can erode their valleys faster than the former can cut water gaps through the mountains. Here at Cowans Gap, Little Aughwick Creek's capture of the stream now flowing north out of Allens Valley must have been quite recent in geologic terms. Prior to this capture Allens Valley drained east through this gap in the Tuscarora Ridge.

You reach Cowans Gap State Park by driving north for 6.4 miles from US 30 on Aughwick Road, by driving south 6.9 miles from US 522 on Burnt Cabins Road, or by driving northwest 3.1 miles from PA 75 on Richmond Road. Once in the park, follow signs to the office, where you can get a booklet describing the hike's points of interest, and then continue on to park at the amphitheater end of the picnic area lot.

To begin, walk down this same road toward the bridge over Little Aughwick Creek, but just before the bridge turn left onto the red-blazed Plessinger Trail. Follow the trail for 1.2 miles (2 km) as it goes upstream between Camping Area A on your left and the creek on your right. At some places the trail divides into several routes. Some follow the stream bank more

Cowans Lake in the gap

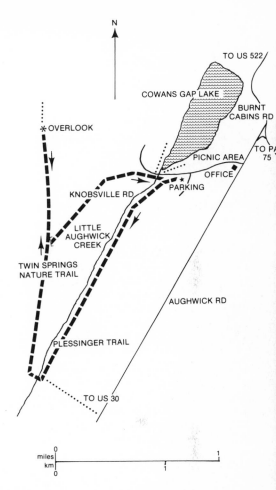

closely than others, but they all rejoin after a bit.

The black gum is a common tree along the trail. Its leaves are not distinctive but the bark of larger trees is deeply furrowed and strongly resembles an alligator hide. The tree's wood is very tough, and in the fall its leaves turn a brilliant scarlet.

Turn right where the red blazes bear sharply left, and cross the bridge over Little Aughwick Creek to the Twin Springs Nature Trail. Two things to

look for on this trail are charcoal flats
or hearths and American chestnut
shoots. The charcoal produced here
was presumably used to smelt iron ore
at Richmond Furnace over in Path
Valley.

The American chestnut has blade-
like leaves with notched edges that
strongly resemble the smooth-edged
leaves of the chestnut oak. At the
turn of the century it was said that
practically every other hardwood
in the Appalachians from Maine to
Georgia was a chestnut. The ideal
forest tree, its nuts could be eaten by
humans and animals. Its wood was
used for everything from fence posts
to window frames. After logging,
chestnut stumps sprouted again
and the new trees grew rapidly.
However, early in this century the
trees contracted a fungal blight from
abroad and were virtually eliminated.
Today the stumps continue to send up
shoots, some of which bear burrs
before they are again felled by the
chestnut blight. The trees' siege is
probably the greatest ecological dis-
aster ever to hit North America.

The Twin Springs Nature Trail ends
at a switchback on the gated Knobsville Road. If the day is reasonably
clear, bear left, uphill, to the overlook
of Cowans Gap and Lake. A fancy
platform at the overlook affords a view
through Cowans Gap into Path Valley.
To end your hike follow the Knobsville
Road back past the vehicle gate and
across the creek to the parking lot.

5 Tuscarora Ridge Trail

Total distance: 4.1 miles (6.5 km)
Walking time: 2½ hours
Vertical rise: 400 feet (125 meters)

Wild azalea

TUSCARORA TUNNEL

PENNSYLVANIA TPKE

TUSCARORA TRAIL

N

TUSCARORA MTN

BUCHANAN STATE FOREST

TO BURNT CABINS

TO FANNETTSBURG AND PA 75

BURNT CABINS RD

PATH VALLEY

PARKING

miles
km
0   1
0   1

by the Civilian Conservation Corps, indicates the trail may have been built by the Corps in the 1930s. The trail is also unusual because it runs along the top of the ridge rather than straight up one side and down the other.

From Exit 14 on the Pennsylvania Turnpike drive south on PA 75 for 2.1 miles to the town of Fannettsburg. Then bear right on Burnt Cabins Road for 2.3 miles to the top of Tuscarora Ridge and the trailhead. Or drive 2.8 miles from US 522 in Burnt Cabins on the same road towards Fannettsburg. Park on the north side of the road or on the south side just west of the crest.

Orange blazes mark the trail; the large white blazes on the trees and rocks here mark the edge of Buchanan State Forest land. Begin walking up the jeep road along a pole line, but then immediately swing left through the woods. At .2 mile (400 meters) a large rock to the right of the trail offers a view over Path Valley and Fannettsburg. Path Valley is named for the Tuscarora Indian path that traversed it. A more extensive view by a large and picturesque white pine lies .1 mile (200 meters) farther on.

Proceed along the trail for a series of views both east and west. At about 2 miles (3.3 km) the good footway ends abruptly. The Tuscarora Trail continues north along the ridge top on an intermittent and obscure path over the Tuscarora Tunnel of the Pennsylvania Turnpike, but it is better to turn back here and retrace your steps to your car.

Wild azalea is uncommon in Penn's Woods but thickets dotted with this delicate flower abound along this trail on the Tuscarora Ridge. The flowers are in bloom the first or second week in May, an ideal time for this hike. This section of one of Pennsylvania's longest trails also boasts excellent views of Path Valley to the east and Burnt Cabins, Cove Mountain, and the southern end of Shade Mountain to the west. The footway here is the best along any ridge-top trail in the state. The crushed sandstone, typically used

6 Little Buffalo State Park

Total distance: 5.7 miles (9.2 km)
Walking time: 3¼ hours
Vertical rise: 330 feet (100 meters)

Little Buffalo Lake

One of the most delightful hikes in the state park system circles a relatively new recreational reservoir in Perry County. Attractions at Little Buffalo State Park in the Juniata Valley also include a covered bridge, a functioning water-powered gristmill, and a twenty-five-post nature trail. A bluebird trail is planned along the route. Alert hikers who see a bird smaller than a robin carrying the sky on its back will recognize the now rare bird loved by Thoreau and so many others. The bluebird trail will consist of many birdhouses arranged along the route. Sparrows and starlings nest earlier than bluebirds so a park system volunteer must inspect the nesting boxes daily during nesting season and evict unwanted tenants. With luck and perseverance a considerable colony of bluebirds may be established.

This hike's terrain is unusually varied, with thick woods on the south giving way to a stream bank and rolling meadows on the north. There are no strenuous climbs, but there is a fair amount of walking up and down hills. Shoes are probably adequate but a few rocky sections and some wet spots make hiking boots preferable. Watch out for poison ivy along the stream. Also, you may want to pick up the nature trail guide at the park office before you begin. The trail is not blazed but is marked with signs at some intersections and is usually well graded and easy to follow.

To reach Little Buffalo State Park, drive south from US 322 at Newport on PA 34 for 2.9 miles to Little Buffalo

Creek Road. Turn right, and then turn left on New Bloomfield Drive, just after park headquarters. Follow the symbols for the hikers' parking lot, which also serves the gristmill.

Begin your hike by the signboard map at the far edge of the parking lot. Bear left on the gravel road between the stream and the lot and then head right to Clay's Bridge. Originally this covered bridge spanned the creek 1 mile (1.6 km) west of this spot. It was moved here when the reservoir dam was built in the early 1970s, and now it carries only foot traffic. Just up the bank on the far side of the bridge you come to Shoaff's Mill, which is slowly being restored. The overshot water wheel was built on this site in 1832.

You now return to a railroad grade you crossed between the bridge and mill and turn left, upstream on the bed of the old Newport and Sherman's Valley Railroad. The narrow-gauge line served this area from the early 1890s to 1929. (At the Path Valley Railroad tunnel in Hike 1 you can see where the attempt to extend this railroad into the next valley came to grief.) Some 200 yards (200 meters) later the old railroad grade goes under the dam, and you turn left to the trail junction and left again onto the nature trail, which makes a switchback up the hillside. This path leads 1.4 miles (2.4 km) through a young hemlock forest and past stump sprouts of native American chestnut, as well as oaks and maples. The charcoal flats you see are reminders that a local iron industry flourished here in the Juniata

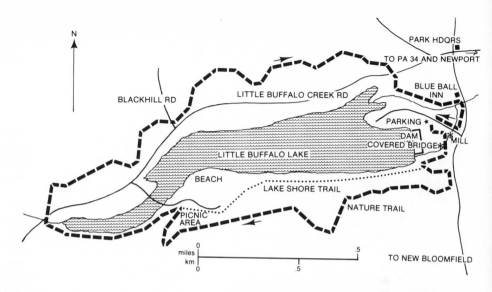

Valley.

Follow the path to a junction in the picnic area, and turn left. (If you wish to return to your car at this point, turn right on the Lake Shore Trail for the 1-mile (1.6-km) walk back to the parking lot.) After a short walk you come to a meadow planted with thousands of pines and hybrid poplars which will, in a few years, become woods.

You next take the mowed path to the right as it swings off the grade and moves along the south bank of Little Buffalo Creek. Walk quietly and you may surprise a bittern or little green heron, or even a great blue heron. The latter may surprise you when it flies off, for it is a sizable bird.

At the end of this stretch turn right on the paved Little Buffalo Creek Road, cross the bridge, and then turn off the road and climb the bank. The trail now winds up through the woods and emerges at the edge of a meadow, where a bench permits rest and a view of the lake and wooded south side. It is along this stretch that the bluebird trail will be built.

As you resume walking through these old fields, you descend to cross tiny brooks that flow to Little Buffalo Creek and other times you range into the woods farther up the slopes. At places the slopes are dry and Virginia pine flourishes, but in the draws the water-loving hemlocks take over.

You may notice a row of chestnut trees at one point beyond Blackhill Road. These are not American chestnuts, but oriental chestnuts planted in the dooryard of a house now gone.

Suddenly the trail leaves the woods for the last time, crosses a field and Little Buffalo Creek Road again. It then parallels the overflow stream from the dam spillway until it reaches the Blue Ball Tavern. This tavern was the halfway house on the turnpike from Carlisle to Sunbury in the early nineteenth century and is now being restored by the Perry County Historical Society.

To bring your hike to an end, turn right on the paved road, cross the creek again, and walk on the grass between the woods and road. Turn right on the next road, which takes you to the parking lot and your car.

Little Buffalo State Park 35

7 Trough Creek

Total distance: 6 miles (9.6 km)
Walking time: 3¼ hours
Vertical rise: 1,300 feet (400 meters)

Hikers visiting this Huntingdon County site will be treated to a mammoth sandstone boulder balanced on the edge of Trough Creek Gorge and an ice mine that produces ice well into the summer. The boulder is termed an "erosion remnant" and probably has not moved very far from where it broke off a rock cliff that has since weathered away. At Copperas Rock, which is also on this hike, you see what may be an earlier stage in this process.

The ice mine is simply a hole in the ground that lies at the base of a slope covered with a thick layer of broken rock. During the winter cold air is drawn in at the base of the slope and cools the rock mass as it rises. In late spring this flow reverses. The cold rocks then chill the air that finally emerges at the base of the slope. In the mine the cold air comes into contact with moist air from the outside and freezes the water vapor on the rocks.

Although this is an enjoyable hike any time, the falls along the way are most spirited in the high water of spring and early summer, but the views become accessible only when the trees have lost their leaves.

To reach the site turn east onto PA 994 from PA 26 between Shy Beaver and Marklesburg. Drive through the village of Entriken, across Raystown Lake, and after 5.3 miles turn north at the sign for Trough Creek State Park. After 1.8 miles bear left on Trough

Footbridge over Trough Creek

Creek Drive for another 3 miles to the former beach parking area. You can also park at Copperas Rock or Laurel Run picnic areas as your hike runs through both. Walking shoes are adequate for this hike.

You begin at the large signboard at the corner of the parking lot. Take the gated service road and footbridge across Trough Creek, climb the bank, and turn right on Old Forge Road. Red blazes mark the Brumbaugh Loop, which you follow over the next 2.5 miles (4 km). After walking along the road less than .2 mile (250 meters), watch for the red blazes heading left up Terrace Mountain. First climbing northwest, you then swing southwest up the ridge line; if the trees are bare you can look to the north and west across Raystown Lake.

Soon you move up the west slope along a confusing stretch in which you go directly across the ridge top and then swing right again. Below the ridge top you continue south along an obscure portion to an old woods road, bear right again down the ridge flank past several other old roads, and bear left on an old dug road that swings down to Old Forge Road. A dug road or trail is one that has been deliberately entrenched for a smoother surface.

Cross the road and continue downhill on the Raven Rock Trail, which swings right, off the road to a house. After about 100 yards (100 meters) turn right uphill (the left-hand trail leads to Trough Creek) to Balanced Rock and a good view of the valley.

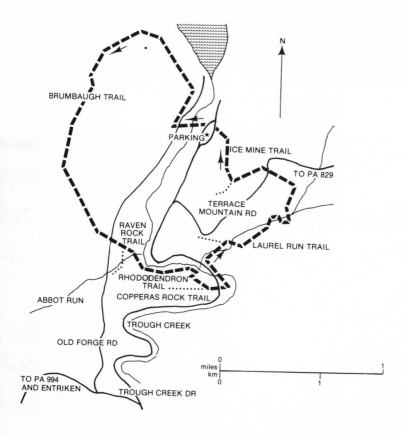

BRUMBAUGH TRAIL

PARKING★

ICE MINE TRAIL

TO PA 829

TERRACE
MOUNTAIN RD

RAVEN
ROCK
TRAIL

LAUREL RUN TRAIL

RHODODENDRON
TRAIL

ABBOT RUN

COPPERAS ROCK TRAIL

TROUGH CREEK

OLD FORGE RD

TO PA 994
AND ENTRIKEN

TROUGH CREEK DR

N

miles
km

0   1

0   1

You then follow Raven Rock Trail
down into Abbot Run and turn sharply
left on Abbot Run Trail. In high water
you might walk up this trail to see
several cascades and waterfalls.

You descend toward the creek, cross
the footbridge, and continue along
Trough Creek on the ledge past the
remains of the suspension bridge. At
this point the way becomes the Rhododendron Trail and continues upstream.
After .3 mile (500 meters) you switch
back up the side of the gorge to the
Copperas Rock Trail junction, turn left
for approximately 100 yards (100
meters), and turn left again on Trough
Creek Drive. Copperas Rock overhangs
the creek beyond the picnic area. Take
the bridge across the creek, swing left
through another picnic area, and, just

beyond the parking lot, turn right on the
Laurel Run Trail. After crossing
Laurel Run five times there is a junction with an old road from the left.
Continue upstream past this junction,
crossing the run four more times, and
then switch back up the side of the
valley. You soon jog left across Terrace Mountain Road.

About .4 mile (600 meters) farther
you bear right at the trail junction and
soon begin the descent into Trough
Creek on the Ice Mine Trail. It leads
gently downhill toward the ice mine,
which stays quite cold through August, long after it has stopped producing ice.

Finish your hike with a left turn on
the paved road and a right turn down
to the parking lot.

8 Sideling Hill

Total distance: 6.2 miles (9.9 km)
Walking time: 3½ hours
Vertical rise: 900 feet (275 meters)

Rock hopping across Roaring Run

Sideling Hill is unusually wide, thus permitting a circuit hike more or less on top of the ridge. The knife edges of Tuscarora, Tussey, and most other ridges do not permit this luxury. The hill's width made Sideling Hill Tunnel the longest of the nine tunnels on W. H. Vanderbilt's South Penn Railway. When work came to a halt in 1885 on "Vanderbilt's Folly" not one of the tunnels had been holed through, and the one at Sideling Hill was the farthest from completion. In the late 1930s Sideling Hill Tunnel was completed—for the Pennsylvania Turnpike instead of a railroad. By the 1960s the two-lane tunnel had become a bottleneck on a four-lane road, and along with the nearby Rays Hill Tunnel it was bypassed when the turnpike was rerouted up and over both ridges.

No views exist along the trail itself, but there is a magnificent one where the hike starts and ends at Sideling Hill Fire Tower on Bald Knob, so-named because trees were slow to vegetate after the knob was logged.

To reach the trail drive east on US 30 from Breezewood 5.5 miles to Sideling Hill. Turn right on Bark Road at the east edge of Sideling Hill picnic area, drive .2 miles, and then bear right on Tower Road. You pass through a colonnade of red pine to reach the base of the fire tower. Park at the side to allow access to the buildings around the clearing.

If the day is clear climb the tower for excellent views of the ridge and valley region. Sideling Hill stretches off to the north and Kimber Mountain hides the strip mines beyond it. Toward the east you see the southern ends of both Jacks and Shade mountains. The Tuscarora ridge and Cove Mountain are also to the east. The high point on Tuscarora, behind the microwave tower, is Big Mountain. To the south Sideling Hill stretches off toward the Mason-Dixon Line and the Potomac. To the west you see Tussey Mountain with a gap, through which pass the Raystown Branch of the Juniata, US 30, and the Pennsylvania Turnpike.

Begin by turning east onto the signed Cliff Trail. The trail moves quickly out of the pine plantation and through a scrubby growth of chestnut oak with many American chestnut sprouts. As you pass by an unmarked trail to the right, Cliff Trail starts its gentle descent to the stream.

About .3 mile (500 meters) farther turn right onto Rock Oak Road. No signs are posted at this junction or the next; the orange diamonds you occasionally see on the trees indicate Rock Oak Road is also a snowmobile trail. When the road forks, bear right as the Cliff Trail goes straight ahead.

A small stream drains into the East Fork of Roaring Run at .9 mile (1.5 km), and at 1.5 miles (2.4 km) you bear right on Roaring Run Trail. This critical junction is marked with a sign reading Rock Oak Road. (Should you miss the junction you will climb Rock Oak Road to Bark Road at the edge of Sideling Hill. In this case turn west on Jackson Trail to avoid retracing your steps.)

If you made the correct turn you

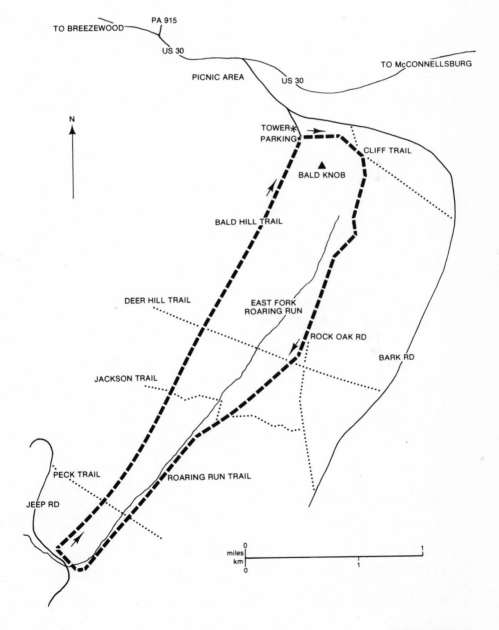

TO BREEZEWOOD
PA 915
US 30
PICNIC AREA
US 30
TO McCONNELLSBURG
N
TOWER
PARKING
CLIFF TRAIL
BALD KNOB
BALD HILL TRAIL
DEER HILL TRAIL
EAST FORK
ROARING RUN
ROCK OAK RD
BARK RD
JACKSON TRAIL
PECK TRAIL
ROARING RUN TRAIL
JEEP RD
miles
km

Sideling Hill 41

cross the signed Deer Hill Trail at 1.6 miles (2.6 km) and Jackson Trail at 2.2 miles (3.6 km). This last junction has new signs identifying both trails, as well as an old metal one from the days of the Civilian Conservation Corps. The CCC sign, which must be over forty years old, was nailed to a tree that has tried to grow around it.

Jackson Trail joins Roaring Run Trail for a bit before turning right. (The hike can be truncated by turning right on either the Deer Hill or Jackson trails and then right again on Bald Hill Trail.) Just before Jackson cuts off, a spring turns the trail muddy for a distance. As you reach the East Fork of Roaring Run the trail tunnels through a dense growth of rhododendron and hemlocks. You cross the stream on stepping stones at 2.5 miles (4 km) and again at 2.9 miles (4.6 km). Now the trail becomes rockier.

You shortly come upon the unsigned Peck Trail, and at 3.4 miles (5.5 km) you turn right on a jeep road and then cross the run on a slab bridge. A short way beyond turn right, *uphill*, on the signed Bald Hill Trail. From here you have nowhere to go but up. At rocky places the footway may vanish but the way is straight and you shouldn't have any trouble picking it up again.

At 3.9 miles (6.3 km) you recross Peck Trail; this time both trails are signed, as are the junctions with Jackson Trail at 4.7 miles (7.6 km) and Deer Hill Trail at 5.4 miles (8.1 km). Soon you cross an unsigned trail, and at 6.1 miles (9.8 km) you reach a gravel road leading to one of the several microwave antennas on Bald Knob. From here it is a short distance to the fire tower and your car.

9 Flat Rock

Total distance: 7 miles (11.2 km)
Walking time: 4 hours
Vertical rise: 1,650 feet (503 meters)

Cumberland Valley from Flat Rock

Natural overlooks are rare in Pennsylvania and trails to them are rarer still. From Flat Rock you are treated to a spectacular view across the Cumberland Valley from one such overlook on the crest of Blue Mountain. This hike is located in Colonel Denning State Park, named for a hero of the American Revolution. The hike traverses the park's length and offers several optional routes as you return from the natural overlook area.

The park is on PA 233 in a valley formed by a hairpin bend of Blue Mountain. To reach it drive 3.4 miles north from the junction with PA 997 at McCrea, or 7.9 miles southwest from the junction with PA 850 at Landisburg.

You begin the Flat Rock Trail at the nature center parking area, which is on the road to the camping area. Cross Doubling Gap Creek on a footbridge (the hike's yellow paint blazes begin here), climb the steps beyond, and then continue on fairly level ground for the next .4 mile (600 meters). Now turn left on a jeep road and start a serious climb. After some 200 yards (200 meters) you pass a spring house; bear right and climb easily for a bit. A final pitch of steep climbing brings you to a major trail junction, the Wagon Wheel, or HUB, atop Blue Mountain. You have traveled a total of 1 mile (1.7 km).

The orange-blazed trail at this intersection is the Tuscarora, which the yellow-blazed Woodburn Trail joins about 60 yards (60 meters) to your right. The yellow-blazed Warner Trail is on your left. At the turn of the century a barrel stave mill operated somewhere near this point. The staves were carried down the mountain by horse and wagon on what is now the Tuscarora Trail.

Continue on Flat Rock Trail across the Wagon Wheel, following yellow blazes. The trail dips gently into Wildcat Hollow and crosses an intermittent run. You then climb to the top of Blue Mountain and, just over the crest, come upon Flat Rock, which has one of the best views in the state. On a clear day you see across the Cumberland Valley to heavily wooded South Mountain. This is the great valley of the Appalachians, extending some 1,900 miles from northern Georgia on your right to Montreal on your left. Be mindful of the drop off the edge of Flat Rock.

Retrace your steps 1 mile (1.6 km) to the Wagon Wheel. You could shorten the hike by continuing straight down the Flat Rock Trail, or taking either the Tuscarora or Woodburn trails now at your left. These lead to PA 233 and you would walk along the highway back to the park. Alternatively you could lengthen the hike by bearing right on the Tuscarora down into Wildcat Hollow, one of the best sections of the Tuscarora Trail. You would have to retrace your steps since this trail does not loop.

Your last choice, and the one this hike takes, bears right on the Warner Trail, which slabs the end of Buck Ridge. You cross over Blue Mountain, wind down into the headwaters of Trout Run, cross a stream, climb to

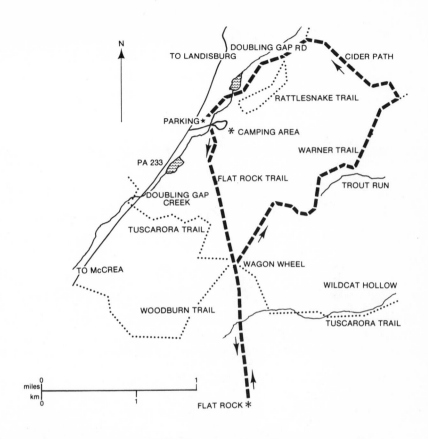

N

TO LANDISBURG
DOUBLING GAP RD
CIDER PATH
RATTLESNAKE TRAIL
PARKING ★
✳ CAMPING AREA
WARNER TRAIL
PA 233
FLAT ROCK TRAIL
TROUT RUN
DOUBLING GAP CREEK
TUSCARORA TRAIL
WAGON WHEEL
TO McCREA
WILDCAT HOLLOW
WOODBURN TRAIL
TUSCARORA TRAIL

0   1
miles
km
0   1
FLAT ROCK ✳

the top of Lays Ridge, and intersect Cider Path. Turn left on this trail for a gentle climb to the top of Blue Mountain. You take a sharp left turn on a newly cut trail at the top of the ridge and walk 50 yards (50 meters) of rocky footway before joining an old log skid. Such skid roads were used to move logs down the mountain. The Cider Path follows the log skid down the ridge, becoming a woods road where it intersects the Doubling Gap Road towards the bottom of the valley. Turn left on Doubling Gap Road for about 200 yards (200 meters) to the park boundary. Before the boundary you can bear left on the white-blazed Rattlesnake Loop Trail, circle the picnic area, and emerge near the dressing

stockade downstream from the beach.

For a direct route to your car, continue along Doubling Gap Road, bear right toward the beach area's far end, cross the creek on the road bridge, and then bear left through the beach parking area. At the far right corner is the end of a Youth Conservation Corps nature trail that takes you back to the nature center and your car.

Backpack camping is permitted on most of the trails outside the park boundaries. Good spots include the spring at the switchback on the Tuscarora Trail west of the Wagon Wheel, along the same trail in Wildcat Hollow, and at the Trout Run headwaters on the Warner Path.

10 Meadow Grounds Lake

Total distance: 7.5 miles (12 km)
Walking time: 4 hours
Vertical rise: 400 feet (120 meters)

Meadow Grounds Mountain stands just west of McConnellsburg in Fulton County. Geologically, this mountain and Scrub Ridge immediately to the west are parts of a syncline of Pocono sandstone. A syncline is the trough formed when layers of rock become folded (the upfolds are anticlines). In this case it is shaped like a canoe about 6 miles (10 km) long. Because the anticlines have eroded faster, the floor of the ridge-girt valley inside this syncline is over 650 feet (200 meters) above the surrounding countryside, In the midst of this hanging valley a small dam has created Meadow Grounds Lake. The lake, and indeed the entire valley are drained by a single stream called Roaring Run. The Pocono sandstone is one of the three major ridge-forming rocks in the state and Roaring Run has cut a steep narrow gap through it. In this passage the run forms many cascades and a waterfall of modest size. Much of this syncline is now part of State Game Lands 53, and two trails have been cleared and marked here in recent years by the Youth Conservation Corps.

To reach the trailhead from McConnellsburg drive west from the junction of US 522 and PA 16 on Lincoln Way for 1 mile and then turn left on LR 29029. After 1.1 miles on this road turn right and follow another road up the flank of Meadow Grounds Mountain. This one swings sharply to the right at the top of the ridge and immediately enters the game lands. Continue

Roaring Run

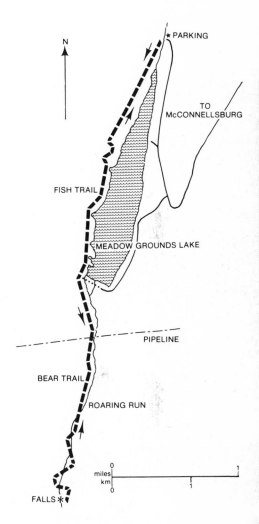

ahead for 1.2 miles more to a small parking area near the lake's north end.

To start your hike walk around the vehicle gate and cross the bridge over Roaring Run, which here is rather placid. At the T junction follow the jeep road to the left, or south, over open meadows that offer repeated

views east over the lake. Some of
these fields are planted for game food
and the hedges of multiflora rose provide cover for small animals.

After 1.1 miles (1.8 km) you enter
the woods and abruptly swing left
toward Meadow Grounds Lake. Just
before the road disappears into the
water turn right on Fish Trail, marked
with yellow fish-shaped blazes. You
proceed through the woods parallel to
the lakeshore for 1.1 miles (1.7 km), to
a junction with Bear Trail at the west
end of the dam forming the lake.

An unblazed trail leads east across
the dam, but your route follows Bear
Trail, marked with yellow bear-shaped
blazes. The trail parallels the overflow
from the spillway and shortly you see
a pond to your left that formed behind
a beaver dam some .4 mile (600 meters) from the trail junction.

You soon cross a pipeline swath,
beyond which Roaring Run begins
moving. Cross the run and bear right
on an old road. Watch for this turn on
your way back as it is easy to miss.
You make five more crossings before
reaching a log bridge for your last one
at the head of the falls. Bear Trail ends
at their bottom.

Retrace your steps for the return to
your car. (The alternate return route
across the rickety bridge over the spillway and around the east side of the
lake only results in some tedious road
walking.)

11 Blue Knob State Park

Total distance: 7.6 miles (12.2 km)
Walking time: 5 hours
Vertical rise: 1,400 feet (425 meters)

Trail marker on ledge

Blue Knob State Park surrounds a knob of unusually high elevation on the Allegheny Front. For many years Blue Knob has had a well-developed system of hiking trails. Some have been abandoned and others downgraded into roads, but it is still possible to enjoy a good day's circuit hike within the park's confines. This pleasant walk through a maturing hardwood forest offers you views of the deeply furrowed Allegheny Front, Dunning Mountain, and other ridges to the east.

The park is 20 miles north of Bedford and the Pennsylvania Turnpike via US 220 and PA 869. In Pavia bear right on LR 07002 into the park. The main road, it passes the park headquarters, the family camping area, and the side road to the fire tower and ski area. If you approach from the north, pick up LR 07002 at the village of Blue Knob and drive south for 5 miles to the park entrance.

Your hike begins on Trail 11 at Campsite 14 in the family camping area. (As this is a circuit hike you can also begin at other points, such as the picnic area at the upper end of Whysong Road or the fire tower. Whysong Road leaves LR 07002 at the park headquarters; the fire tower is on the left, off the side road to the ski area.) While hiking boots are recommended, you will fare well with any good walking shoes.

Trail 11, marked with a white 11 and the red blaze of the Lost Turkey Trail, (see Hike 47) runs from Campsite 14 along an old road through open woods

skirting the edge of the camp area. Soon you pass a post marked with a 2, which indicates you are now only 2 kilometers (1.2 miles) from the fire tower and the start of the Lost Turkey Trail. After .9 mile (1.4 km) of level hiking, Trail 11 turns right uphill off the old road. There's a good spring on the old road at this corner.

After a short climb you emerge at a junction of paved roads. Follow the left road for about 50 yards (50 meters) and then turn right on Tower Trail, which is still Trail 11. You now climb steeply over a series of switchbacks. Toward the top you encounter well-made stone steps, but trees have grown in front of the lookout point, obscuring the view. Continue to the top of Herman Point and bear left in the clearing to Blue Knob fire tower. If the weather is clear climb the tower for a view in all directions, including Blue Knob to the southeast and the installations at the top of the ski slope.

From here the circuit hike descends the paved tower access road and bears left, uphill, on the paved road to the ski area. This climb is out in the open—hot on sunny days—but there's no alternative.

After climbing almost .4 mile (600 meters) bear right on a gated gravel road at the hairpin bend where you find an electrical substation. (If you want to see the view from Blue Knob itself continue to the end of the paved road and bear left among the buildings to the top of the ski lift. Dunning, Loop, and Lock mountains, and if the weather is good Tussey Mountain, are

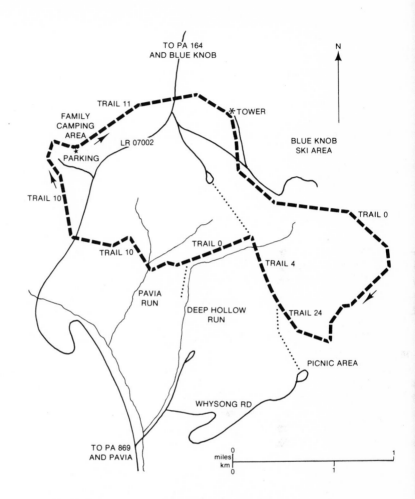

TO PA 164
AND BLUE KNOB

N

TRAIL 11

FAMILY
CAMPING
AREA

★
PARKING

LR 07002

✳ TOWER

BLUE KNOB
SKI AREA

TRAIL 10

TRAIL 10

TRAIL 0

TRAIL 0

TRAIL 4

TRAIL 24

PAVIA
RUN

DEEP HOLLOW
RUN

PICNIC AREA

WHYSONG RD

TO PA 869
AND PAVIA

miles
km

0

0

1

1

visible on the horizon. During the ski season, snacks are available. To continue the hike retrace your steps to the substation.)

The gravel road has obliterated parts of Trails 0 and U, but blazes for both can still be found near the start. Ignore them and follow the road for the next 1 mile (1.6 km). At a turn just above the park water supply go straight ahead on a jeep road; then shortly turn right again on another switchback. Here you are on Trail 0 where you

follow the blazes again. In places this jeep road, which is a snowmobile trail in winter, is practically cut into the face of the cliff. Both the lookouts marked on the park map are overgrown but at one point you get a peephole view across Deep Hollow.

After another 1 mile (1.7 km) Trail 0 diverges right and Trail 3 dives to the left. Ignore them and proceed on the jeep road, which now descends and is called Trail 24A.

About .3 mile (500 meters) farther,

turn right on Trail 4. The picnic area at the top of Whysong Road is about 200 yards (200 meters) left of this junction. Trail 4, another jeep road, is easy, level walking. After another .6 mile (1 km) the trail goes across Deep Hollow Run, where you may find water. A short distance beyond, watch closely for Trail 0 to the left.

Turn left on Trail 0 and descend along a section of the group camp. After the camp area the way is a bit overgrown but easy to follow. About .2 mile (300 meters) beyond bear right on what is now Trails 10 and 0 combined. In another .2 mile (400 meters) turn sharply right on Trail 10 and descend to Pavia Run. You have no footway here, so watch the blazes carefully. Trail 10 turns left downstream for nearly 100 yards (100 meters) before crossing to a junction with Trail 1. Stay on Trail 10 and 100 yards (100 meters) later you see a dirt floor Adirondack-type shelter with a spring and outhouse to the right. This shelter is for emergency use only, since back-packing is not permitted in the park.

Trail 10 now climbs steeply past the shelter and continues upward for the next .2 mile (400 meters). After slab-bing the side of the hill for .4 mile (600 meters) it meets Trail 104 at a confus-ing junction. Trail 10, which you stay on, does not descend but jogs right and continues on an old road grade.

You soon cross the paved road (LR 07002). Your climb is over and the trail is clear on this side of the road. It is only another .6 mile (900 meters) back to your hike's start.

12 Terrace Mountain Trail

Total distance: 7.7 miles (12.4 km)
Walking time: 4 hours
Vertical rise: 1,000 feet (305 meters)

Tatman Run access area on Raystown Lake

In 1973 the Corps of Engineers completed a flood-control dam on the Raystown Branch of the Juniata River in Huntingdon County and in the process acquired 21,000 acres of surrounding land. Together with adjacent lands of Rothrock State Forest, here designated as the Trough Creek Wild Area, virtually the entire western flank of Terrace Mountain was brought into public ownership.

Terrace Mountain Trail follows the mountain just to the east of Raystown Lake. Currently the trail is complete from Weaver Bridge north to Trough Creek State Park. Further extensions north are planned, but the completed portion provides an excellent day hike or an easy, leisurely introduction to backpacking using either of the primitive camping areas, accessible by boat, which lie nearby. These areas have well water, picnic tables, and pit toilets. By backpacking standards they are fairly palatial.

A car shuttle is required for a day hike on this part of Terrace Mountain Trail. You reach the trailhead by driving east on PA 994 from PA 26 for 4.7 miles. Turn left to the Tatman Run Access Area, and drive another 1.4 miles to a small parking area atop a hill overlooking Raystown Lake. Leave one car here. Drive back to PA 994 and turn left. Drive .6 mile and take a sharp right on a paved road at a sign for Trough Creek State Park. Continue on this road through Little Valley for 6.4 miles to Middletown, where you bear right on PA 912 for .9 mile. Then turn right again at a sign for the

Weaver Falls Access Area. Another 1.1 miles brings you to the east end of Weaver Bridge and the south end of Terrace Mountain Trail. A few cars can be parked here without blocking the gate and more space is available on the bridge's far side.

Walk around the gate and head north on Terrace Mountain Trail. The first stretch is just barely above the recreation lake level and would be inundated in the event of a flood. Raystown Dam is a multipurpose dam for both recreation and flood control.

Along here you follow the old Tressler jeep road, still used as a management road but gated to other vehicles. The absence of motorcycle tracks shows a commendable level of enforcement. After .4 mile (700 meters) you swing right, away from the lake, and climb over a small hill at an inside bend in the lake. By 1.4 miles (2.2 km) you are back at the lakeside, but after another .6 mile (1 km) you enter state forest lands to climb away from the water again. This time you continue to climb until, at 2.7 miles (4.4 km), you reach a side trail leading left to Putts Camp, .6 mile (1 km) down the flank of Terrace Mountain.

You continue climbing easily and finally reach an elevation almost 400 feet (120 meters) above the lake. In June, jack-in-the-pulpits grow along this stretch. You make a gentle descent to lake level and at 4.7 miles (7.6 km) reach a side trail left to the Peninsula Camp, .2 mile (300 meters) off the trail.

At 5.6 miles (9 km) you turn right

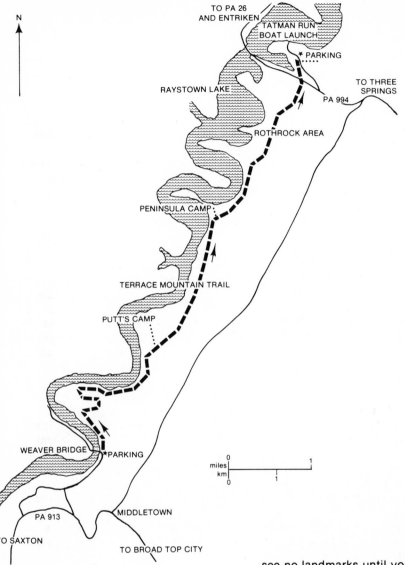

N

TO PA 26
AND ENTRIKEN

TATMAN RUN
BOAT LAUNCH

* PARKING

RAYSTOWN LAKE

TO THREE
SPRINGS

PA 994

ROTHROCK AREA

PENINSULA CAMP

TERRACE MOUNTAIN TRAIL

PUTT'S CAMP

WEAVER BRIDGE

*Parking

MIDDLETOWN

PA 913

TO SAXTON

TO BROAD TOP CITY

miles
km

0   1

0   1

see no landmarks until you turn right
on an old road at 7 miles (11.2 km).

You cross PA 994 at 7.1 miles (11.5
km) and then follow switchbacks down
to Tatman Run, which you cross via
the bridge. You continue down this
valley and climb to the Tatman Run
access road. Bear left for the short
distance to the parking area and your
car.

into the woods on a newly cut orange-
blazed trail and thus avoid the Rothrock Camping Area, open only to
campers occupying the 200 sites. You
soon cross a road leading uphill to a
small reservoir and from here on you

13 Martin Hill Wild Area

Total distance: 9.1 miles (14.6 km)
Walking time: 5 hours
Vertical rise: 1,610 feet (490 meters)

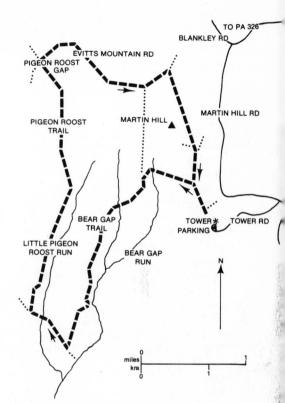

Tussey Mountain reaches its highest elevation at Martin Hill. At 2,775 feet (846 meters) you're not likely to experience altitude sickness but this looks to be the highest elevation in the Appalachian ridge and valley region. Together with the adjacent Sweet Root Natural Area, a total of 13,000 acres of this rugged mountain has been designated wild area. The Martin Hill Wild Area extends south nearly 10 miles (16 km) to the Mason-Dixon Line.

To reach the trailhead drive south from Bedford on PA 326 and at the hilltop just beyond Rainsburg turn right on Blankley Road. After 2.2 miles bear left on Martin Hill Road for 1.9 miles; then turn right on Tower Road for approximately 1 mile to the Martin Hill fire tower. In parking do not block access to the microwave and radio antennas.

If weather permits, tower views to the south include Tussey and Evitts mountains flanking Bean's Cove, with Martin Hill forming a high ridge between them. To the north the mountains separate and flank Friend's Cove. The break in Tussey just to the northeast is Sweet Root Gap.

To start, head north along the Evitts Mountain jeep road past the large microwave installation and then Basin Trail on the right. At .4 mile (670 meters) turn left on a gated but unnamed woods road—the first trail to the left after the microwave installation.

Make a gentle descent and cross

Martin Hill fire tower

Bear Gap Run; then climb steeply to a junction with Bear Gap Trail at 1 mile (1.6 km), where you head left and continue the descent south toward Bean's Cove. Cross Little Bear Gap Run, continue past two old roads on the left at 2.5 miles (4.1 km), and move ahead to a small clearing, in the midst of which a small tulip tree grows, and the junction with Pigeon Roost Trail.

Turn right on this trail, which leads past Pigeon Roost Spring; then bear left when the old woods road forks and cross Little Pigeon Roost Run. You pass a shale pit and at 3.3 miles (5.3 km) bear right at another fork. Note the left fork continues along the hill base. Climb slowly to a false summit at 4.4 miles (7.1 km), where the trail levels and you can see Evitts Mountain above. Bear right at another fork at 5.2 miles (8.4 km). At 5.9 miles (9.5 km) you pass a vehicle gate and reach the Evitts Mountain jeep road at Pigeon Roost Gap.

The pigeons that roosted here were probably the now-extinct passenger pigeons. These birds migrated in great flocks and frequently returned to the same roosts each year. They were hunted for the market and exterminated despite their great numbers.

Turn right on Evitts Mountain Road and continue climbing the broad summit of Martin Hill, passing Bear Gap Trail on your right at 7.3 miles (11.7 km), Cabin Trail on your left, the gated Bear Gap Drive on the right, and Refuge Trail on the left. At 8.6 miles (13.8 km) you see an open area off to the left. Push through the brush to the top of a scree slope for a view of Sweet Root Gap.

Return to the Evitts Mountain Road and continue for the .4 mile (700 meters) back to Martin Hill fire tower and your car.

14 State Game Land 211

Total distance: 9.2 miles (14.8 km)
Walking time: 4½ hours
Vertical rise: 1,200 feet (365 meters)

View to Clark Valley

The largest roadless area in Pennsylvania is the setting for this hike. State Game Land 211, only 12 miles from Harrisburg, covers 35,000 acres. But this region was not always wild. Iron furnaces burned here in pre-Revolutionary days, and the area is dotted with ghost towns such as Rausch Gap and Yellow Springs. The Schuylkill and Susquehanna Railroad provided rail service to communities such as Cold Spring, and logging operations as well as underground and surface coal mining have taken place here.

To reach the trailhead drive east from PA 225 in Dauphin on Stony Creek Road, immediately adjacent to the creek. Bear right onto the old railroad grade when you reach the turnaround at the end of the paved road. East of this point Stony Creek Road follows the old Schuylkill and Susquehanna Railroad grade. Park anywhere after you pass the Rattling Run Road junction, 6 miles from Dauphin.

Begin walking west, back to a pipeline swath, over the road you just traveled. Bear right uphill with the pipeline, and then right again on the Rattling Run Road. This was a stage road at the time of the Revolution. You pass the steel gate, swing northeast, and begin climbing Third Mountain. Toward the top you walk a level road along which lies a piped spring that flows even in August. This area also offers views to the south and west.

A side road runs left to a radio tower atop Third Mountain. Continuing on Rattling Run Road you pass extensive game food plots. After 1.2 miles (2 km) the road diverges; bear left to Stony Mountain fire tower, now visible down the road.

The view from the fire tower is truly spectacular. To the east is Saint Anthony's Wilderness, Rattling Run Gap, and Third Mountain split into Stony Mountain to the north and Sharp Mountain to the south. Stony Creek Valley is obscured by Third Mountain, but to the north you can see De Hart Reservoir, the public water supply for Harrisburg. To the west the Susquehanna cuts between Peters Mountain and Cove Mountain. The view south is of Second and Blue mountains and beyond them the Furnace Hills on the far side of Cumberland Valley.

This view and great tract of wild land are threatened. Pennsylvania Power and Light and Metropolitan Edison have obtained possession of a vast inholding for the construction of a pumped storage project. A dam on Stony Creek would produce a lower reservoir the size of De Hart Reservoir. A smaller upper reservoir is planned immediately to the east of the tower on the high ground between Sharp and Stony mountains. Pennsylvania Power and Light land extends almost to the tower base. Is it really necessary that a pumped storage project be built in the middle of the largest roadless area in the state?

From your perch in the fire tower you may see vultures and hawks riding the ridge wave above Third Mountain. You can distinguish them by their wings: vultures have an angled wing while hawks, like eagles, hold their

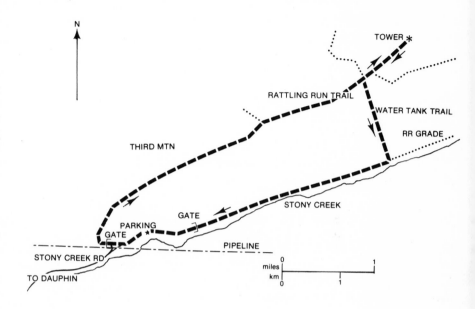

wings in a straight line.

On descending the fire tower retrace your steps to Rattling Run Road. Bear right, passing two small ponds on your left and a clearing on your right, and then turn left onto the Water Tank Trail along the west side of the clearing. No footway is evident at first but after you cross a small stream from the left a rocky grade appears. Follow it down the south flank of Third Mountain. This grade which is similar to that at the Allegheny Portage Railroad (Hike 20) but steeper, was built to transport timber from Clark Valley north of Third Mountain to the Schuylkill and Susquehanna Railroad in Stony Valley.

Toward the bottom of the incline you get a better footway by bearing left on an old road a short distance.

Where the road swings back across the incline bear left again down the rocky grade.

When you reach the old Schuylkill and Susquehanna Railroad grade, turn right. Trails to the south, worn by fishermen, lead to Stony Creek. Bicyclists you may see on this grade are likely to be fishermen, hunters—or persons attracted by the lack of automobiles along the 18-mile (29-km) stretch. Bikes with balloon tires work better than those with narrow ones, which sink in the trail surface. This must be one of the most delightful bicycle rides in the state, but it will be shortened if the pumped storage project is built.

Continue back to the starting point and your car.

15 John P. Saylor Memorial Trail

Total distance: 12.3 miles (19.8 km)
Walking time: 6½ hours
Vertical rise: 400 feet (120 meters)

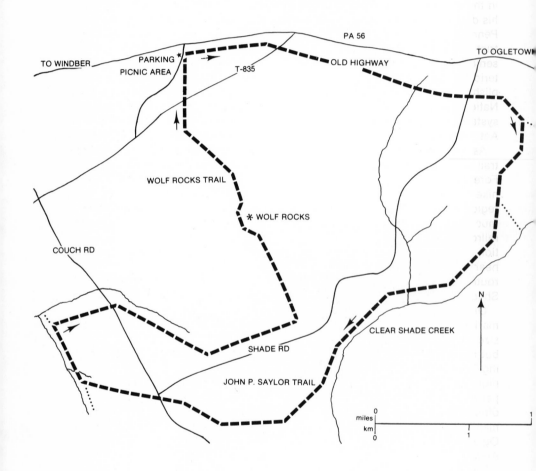

TO WINDBER

PARKING
PICNIC AREA

T-835

PA 56

OLD HIGHWAY

TO OGLETOWN

WOLF ROCKS TRAIL

* WOLF ROCKS

COUCH RD

CLEAR SHADE CREEK

N

SHADE RD

JOHN P. SAYLOR TRAIL

miles 0 — 1
km 0 — 1

John P. Saylor became one of the great conservationists of our time during the twenty-four years he served in the U.S. Congress. From 1949 until his death in 1973 he represented Pennsylvania's Twenty-Second District and for many years he was the senior Republican on the House Interior Committee. Among his accomplishments are sponsorship of the National Wilderness Preservation system and the National Scenic Trails Act. We are all in his debt.

As a memorial to Saylor a hiking trail has been blazed in Gallitzen State Forest in Somerset County. While the hike is long, traveling is easy since this region is on the Allegheny Plateau and much of the trail follows old roads and railroad grades. The only rough section is in the vicinity of Wolf Rocks near the trail's end. Nearly half the route traverses the 2,791-acre Clear Shade Wild Area.

Orange rectangles are used as markers. Blue blazes of the same size are posted on parts of the trail, but these mark the Babcock Ski Touring Trail. If you wish to camp overnight along the trail, obtain a free permit from either the district forest office in Ebensburg or the forest foreman headquarters on PA 56 between Ogletown and the Babcock Picnic Area.

The hike begins in the Babcock Picnic Area on PA 56 between Ogletown and Windber, where there is ample parking. Starting at the large sign, turn left and follow the trail along the edge of the picnic area. Fill your canteen as you pass the water pump since the few springs along the trail may be dry. The trail bears right on old PA 56, which was the original wagon road between Bedford and Johnstown. Before that it was the Conemaugh Indian Path.

About .6 mile (1 km) from the start you cross a paved road. After this the old road is gated and walking becomes more enjoyable. At 2 miles (3.2 km), you cross Shade Road and enter the Clear Shade Wild Area. As with most road crossings on this trail, it is gated to prevent vehicular traffic.

After another .4 mile (600 meters) turn right onto a grassed-over timber haul road, where selective cutting operations were conducted in 1962 and 1963 before the Wild Area was established. The old haul road is again easy walking.

In 1.2 miles (2 km) you turn right again, enter a band of extensive meadows along Clear Shade Creek, and then pick up an old logging railroad grade used by the Babcock Lumber Company around the turn of the century.

You can tell you are on an old railroad grade by the occasional small fills and cuts required to keep the grade constant for steam locomotives. The meadows are caused by soil erosion, old forest fires, and probably by a high water table along the nearby creek. These meadows and their woodland boundaries provide a diversity of wildlife habitats.

Some distance along you cross a large stream on a log bridge; an unblazed trail to the left leads to the ruins of a splash dam on Clear Shade Creek. You can hear the water falling from where you stand on the main trail. Would you guess the water-soaked boards you see here have been in place since the last century? A splash dam was built then in order to float logs down this stream, which otherwise would have been too small for a log drive even during the spring runoff.

Just past 5 miles (8 km) you bear right off the old railroad grade, bypass a wet spot once bridged by a high trestle, and start the climb out of the Clear Shade watershed. You soon rejoin the old railroad grade, which now climbs gently toward the plateau. This is the halfway point on the trail. After passing through more meadows, you cross Couch Road.

Immediately after crossing this road, the Saylor Trail bears right on another railroad grade down into a hollow towards Sandy Run. After crossing three different water courses, which are probably intermittent this far up, you turn right, leaving the railroad grade for good, and soon pick up an old woods road that winds gently upward to Couch Road again.

After you recross Couch Road you hit the first lengthy section of real trail, which continues climbing gently to the edge of a meadow. A slab-sided shelter has been built but does not appear attractive for camping. Turn left through the meadow, past the site of Logging Camp 59, which was used by the Babcock Lumber Company around 1900.

At the meadow's end you bear right and wind through the woods on a new trail which has little or no footway. The way becomes rougher and rockier and finally turns right onto the well-worn Wolf Rocks Trail. Once extensive views may have been available from the top of these rocks, but the trees have grown high and the views are disappointing. The Wolf Rocks site is an eloquent argument for banning spray paint. These are the most vandalized rocks I have ever seen.

You now descend the rough trail past a spring at the base of Wolf Rocks, and after .6 mile (1 km) follow the trail under a pole line and jog right across a paved road. You cross two more streams, the first over a log bridge, before returning to the picnic area and your car.

Middle District

16 Alan Seeger Trail

Total distance: 1.2 miles (2 km)
Walking time: ½ hour
Vertical rise: None

In the Seven Mountains region of Central Pennsylvania grows a small stand of old hemlocks known as the Alan Seeger Natural Area. In 1921, Colonel Henry Shoemaker, then a member of the Pennsylvania State Forest Commission, chose to name this area for a young American poet who was killed in France in World War I. According to Alan Seeger's biography, he never ventured any closer to Pennsylvania than Staten Island. Curiously though, a state forest map of the Seven Mountains dated February 1920 shows several sites with variations of the Seeger name, all of them to the north and west of the natural area. The poet's relationship to these places is unknown, as is Shoemaker's reason for the commemoration.

You reach the Alan Seeger Natural Area by driving west on the mostly paved Stone Creek Road 7.3 miles from US 322 at Laurel Creek Reservoir or by traveling 6.4 miles east from PA 26 at McAlevys Fort.

You begin walking the trail at the sign in the parking area next to the junction of the Stone Creek and Seeger roads. Another sign says the trail takes only fifteen minutes to walk, but it's worth your while to take longer. The trail first winds through open woods. Many of the trees and shrubs along the way are identified by signs, which makes this an ideal walk for those who are still learning which is which. Among them are black birch,

Alan Seeger Trail lined with rhododendron

white oak, pitch pine, flowering dogwood, and red maple.

In about .3 mile (450 meters) the path intersects the Greenwood Spur of the Mid State Trail system (see Hike 28). If you turn left and walk a short distance down the spur and across Stone Creek Road you encounter one of the mysteries of this area: the grade of a narrow-gauge railroad. The grade is the remnant of a logging railroad that led to Milroy and was used by several lumber companies around the turn of the century. The mystery lies in how the big trees in this area were spared in the logging operations, and even earlier in the widespread charcoal operation from Greenwood Iron Furnace on the far side of Broad Mountain. Charcoal flats can be found far up Grass Mountain beyond Alan Seeger. Why was this area bypassed?

Retrace your steps to the junction, continue straight on the Alan Seeger Trail, and head toward the rhododendrons. In places these hardy bushes are twenty feet high and arch over the trail, creating a green tunnel. They are usually in full bloom the first week of July, making that an ideal time to hike this route. Off the trail, the jungle of rhododendrons is fully as impenetrable as it looks.

About halfway around the loop you come on some of the oldest trees in the state. Secure on their island in Stone Creek, they must have survived the summer of 1644 when most of Pennsylvania is believed to have burned over.

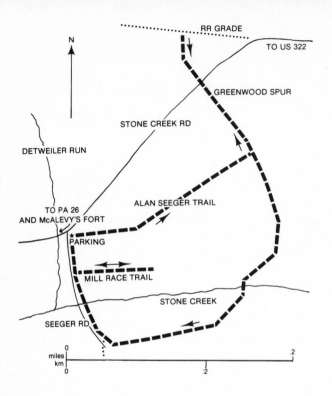

Nobody knows just how old these trees really are, but they are considerably larger than the 500-year-old hemlock lying across Mill Race Trail farther along this hike. Age estimates are based on their size with respect to other hemlocks in the same area that have been dated by ring counting. Since they are over twice the diameter of the Mill Race tree, 600 years is a very conservative estimate. The full extrapolation is 1,200 years, and that's the best number we'll have until these trees die or fall over. Nobody is going to risk damaging them by taking a core sample. If they really are 1,200 years old, they would rival the box huckleberry in Perry County as the oldest living things in Penn's Woods.

Unlike jack pines, whose cones open only with the heat of a forest fire, hemlocks are dependent on living trees to seed a new generation. Presumably most of the hemlocks in the Seven Mountains are descended from these specimens.

After crossing a footbridge over Stone Creek you bear right again through open woods. Shortly you arrive at Seeger Road, where the Greenwood Spur turns to the left, up Johnson Trail. Bear right on the road, following it back across Stone Creek to Mill Race Trail, where a right turn brings you to the 500-year-old hemlock. It has been dated by actual ring counting. The millrace from which this trail takes its name carried water to a water-powered sawmill believed to have been called Milligan Mills. So, with the charcoal operations and a sawmill on one side and a logging railroad on another, the survival of this area's hemlocks becomes a triple mystery.

You now retrace your steps to the road. A short distance to your right is the parking area, where there are picnic tables and shelters. A hand pump is on the far side of Detweiler Run.

17 Wykoff Run Natural Area

Total distance: 3.4 miles (5.4 km)
Walking time: 2 hours
Vertical rise: 120 feet (35 meters)

Butterflies dining on thistle

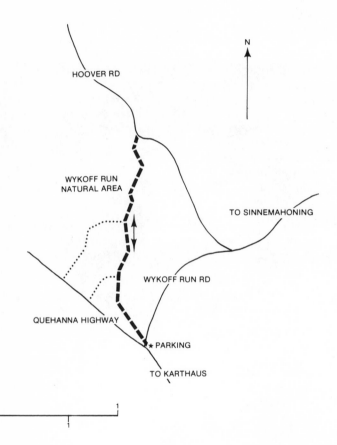

Wykoff Run Natural Area in the
50,000-acre Quehanna Wild Area
near Karthaus was established to pre-
serve a beautiful stand of white birch.
But as you drive to the trailhead and
take this short, easy hike, you see
evidence of other use before the legis-
lature declared it the state's largest
wild area.

The state made heroic efforts to
attract industry to this part of Cam-
eron County when it showed signs of
economic recession after World War II
and was successful with the Curtiss-
Wright Aircraft Company, which
wanted a secluded area to build
jet engines and experiment with
nuclear-powered aircraft. To satisfy
the company's requirements, hunting
camps were removed from a 50,000-
acre tract of state forest land and entrance was forbidden to all outsiders.

But things went badly for Curtiss-Wright. The region's unemployed coal miners knew nothing about jet engines and nuclear-powered aircraft, so engineers and scientists were imported to work and to live in the company town of Pine Glen. The industrial venture soon failed. Curtiss-Wright abandoned the jet engine field and nuclear-powered aircraft went undeveloped. Today the Piper Aircraft Company uses a few buildings at the main gate, and a four-megawatt research reactor stands in the woods but has been dormant since the 1960s. The rest of the area has reverted to deer, bears, and occasional hikers.

To reach the trailhead, drive up the Quehanna Highway from PA 879 in Karthaus for 8.7 miles to the junction with paved Wykoff Run Road, or drive 9.9 miles on Wykoff Run Road from PA 120 at Sinnemahoning. There is parking space for several cars at the junction of the two roads.

The blue-blazed trail, also a ski-touring trail, bisects the angle between the two roads. Some .4 mile (600 meters) from your start, you cross a dry run and a short distance beyond enter a clearing. Here stands a concrete building once used to store hazardous or explosive materials. Continue ahead and cross another small stream, probably the headwaters of Wykoff Run.

At 1 mile (1.6 km) you pass an unblazed woods road on the left. Move straight ahead with the blazes for the best of the trail—mountain laurel and large white birch on both sides. At about 1.2 miles (1.9 km) you see a large clearing to the left, and at 1.7 miles (2.7 km) you reach Hoover Road, where the ski trail turns right. You now retrace your steps and return to your car.

18 Snyder Middleswarth State Park

Total distance: 3.4 miles (5.4 km)
Walking time: 2 hours
Vertical rise: 760 feet (230 meters)

An extensive stand of old growth timber along Swift Run in Bald Eagle State Forest is the setting for this hike. The trees are protected because they fall within the boundaries of the Snyder Middleswarth National Natural Landmark and the Tall Timbers Natural Area, parts of a 14,000-acre tract in Snyder County purchased by the state in 1902. Most of the big trees are hemlocks and a few are white pine. Because hemlock is brittle and may shatter when sawed into boards, it is not a profitable tree to log. This fact may have contributed to the owners' willingness to part with such a large tract containing hundreds of uncut acres.

The hike begins in Snyder Middleswarth State Park, an eight-acre area of the state forest set aside for picnicking and parking. To reach the trailhead, turn north off PA 235 in in Troxelville onto Swift Run Road, where there's a large sign for the park. Follow Swift Run Road for 4.7 miles to the entrance and parking area. Walking shoes are fine for the hike's good trail and short stretch of road.

You begin hiking on the Swift Run Trail, which leads upstream from the parking area, and immediately encounter the big trees. Bypass the trail on your left at .4 mile (670 meters), which leads back to the parking on the opposite bank of Swift Run.

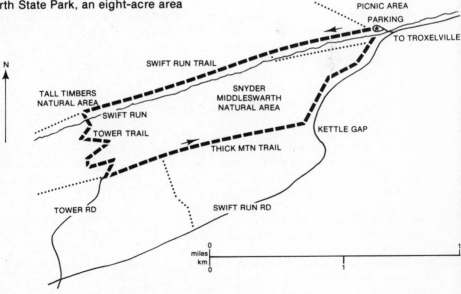

Swift Run Trail

After 1.2 miles (2 km) Tower Trail cuts off to the left across Swift Run. This critical junction is marked by a small metal sign on the right. (Should you miss it, you will see the big trees come to an abrupt end in .3 mile (500 meters). The trail then deteriorates rapidly, is overgrown with mountain laurel, and fringed with scrubby virgin timber. In another 2.5 miles (4 km) the trail reaches the west end of Tall Timbers Natural Area.)

Bearing left onto Tower Trail, you cross Swift Run on some rocks and start up the north flank of Thick Mountain. Bear right on the first switchback. The switchbacks are in good shape and offer easier climbing than the cutoff, which is starting to erode. This is the only real climb on the hike.

At the ridge top you see four foundation posts at the end of a road. They are all that remain of Snyder Middleswarth fire tower. Views from the tower must have been fine, but the structure was a victim of state economy measures and the vandalism that still afflicts other towers.

You now turn left on Thick Mountain Trail (the sign mistakenly calls it Tall Timbers Trail), follow the crest of the ridge for .2 mile (400 meters), and then pass an unnamed trail to the right. You begin your descent into Kettle Gap, moving from a gradual to steep slope fairly rapidly. Toward the bottom you bear left on an old road grade and then cross an underground stream. You can hear the water flowing under the rocks.

The trail brings you out onto Swift Run Road, and you should turn left downhill. Walk about .3 mile (500 meters) and turn left on the road into Snyder Middleswarth picnic area. Cross Swift Run and you are back at your car.

19 Blair Trail

Total distance: 3.9 miles (6.3 km)
Walking time: 2¼ hours
Vertical rise: 200 feet (60 meters)

Marsh marigolds

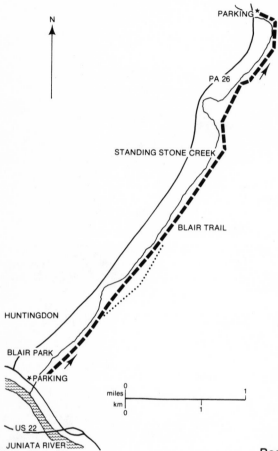

Residents of Huntingdon are fortunate to have a hiking trail of unusual quality that may also be the state's oldest purely recreational trail. Blair Trail starts in Blair Park at the edge of town and proceeds far into the surrounding countryside. The shielding effects of vegetation and topography insulate the trail from development. To the west the trail is paralleled by PA 26 on the far side of Standing Stone Creek, and to the east it is bordered by Ridge Road on the top of Stone Creek Ridge.

But the Blair Trail is more than a happy accident of geography. It dates back to the latter part of the nineteenth century when, through the generosity of Mrs. Kate F. Blair, it was built for nature lovers who walked, bicycled, or drove their carriages as far as Blue Hole.

Today, through the cooperation of public-spirited landowners and concerned citizens, the trail has been reopened to foot travel and extended to a junction with PA 26. Trail users must now do their part to insure the route stays open. If you find litter along the trail try to find room for it in your pockets or pack. Stay on the trail and report any vandalism or motorized use of the trail to the Standing Stone Garden Club in Huntingdon. Remember, the Blair Trail is entirely on private land and any single landowner could sever it for good.

This hike utilizes a car shuttle which, of course, requires two or more cars. Spot the first car by driving north on PA 26 for 3.7 miles from Blair Park to .1 mile beyond the first bridge over Standing Stone Creek. Park on the road edge near a dirt ramp leading into an evergreen plantation. In the other car drive back to Huntingdon and turn in next to the Foodliner, circle around the water company building, and park in the large area behind it. If you use only one car and retrace your steps, remember to double the total distance and time noted here.

To begin, walk downstream next to the beach and cross the bridge over Standing Stone Creek. Turn left at the first gate on the far side and walk past a few picnic tables; you are now on the Blair Trail.

Continue straight ahead past an old road on the right at .2 mile (400 meters). At .8 mile (1.3 km) the trail splits into a low road and a high road. They are exactly the same length and rejoin after .7 mile (1.1 km). You might prefer the low road as much of the high trail's view is obscured when the trees are in leaf. Some of the white pines and hemlocks are of pretty fair

size, but the special treats of this trail are the wildflowers on the forest floor. The marsh marigold, trout lily, skunk cabbage, hepatica, and bluet are at their best in late April or early May.

At 2.7 miles (4.3 km) the trail drops to a low area on an inside bend in Standing Stone Creek, Blue Hole. Named after a deep spot in the creek, it was the terminus of the old carriage road that was the original Blair Trail. There are a variety and abundance of wildflowers here. You now continue on a narrow footpath that is a bit obscure at first but becomes more evident along the base of the slope ahead.

At 2.9 miles (4.7 km) you pass under a single power line on wooden poles and at 3.2 miles (5.2 km) cross a much larger swath with two power lines on steel pylons. Finally, at 3.7 miles (5.9 km), you descend again to the creek and briefly follow the bank, bearing right through the plantation of red pine and Norway spruce to emerge at the edge of PA 26, where your second car is parked.

20 Allegheny Portage Railroad

Total distance: 4 miles (6.4 km)
Walking time: 3 hours
Vertical rise: 575 feet (175 meters)

Don't be put off by the contemporary look of the wood-chip surfacing on two of the three trails on this hike. A great deal of history lies along them, and they may even hold lessons about today's technology.

The portage railway was the 1820's solution to getting a canal over a mountain. Today we realize Pennsylvania officials should have built a proper railroad from Philadelphia to Pittsburgh to compete with the Erie and Chesapeake and Ohio canals. But the railroads of that day were puny—they couldn't climb the grades carrying the weight loaded canal boats could. The building of the Pennsylvania Canal was the prudent choice; but the rapid development of railroads made the canal and portage system obsolete within twenty years of its completion—not long enough to pay off the bonds that had been sold to finance the project. Nevertheless, canals did cut the shipping time from Philadelphia to Pittsburgh from over three weeks by wagon to only 3½ days.

The Allegheny portage railroad system, developed to get the canal over the Allegheny Mountains, included an ascent of 1,380 feet (420 meters) at the end of the Juniata Canal at Hollidaysburg. Stationary steam engines pulled the railroad cars up a series of ten inclines. (There are no weight restrictions on a stationary engine and also no traction problems.) The inclines had grades of from four percent to six

View up Incline 8

percent, but unlike those for a railroad they had to be straight. Hemp ropes were used initially, but incidences of runaway loads resulted in the switch to steel ropes. On levels between inclines cars could be pulled by horses, but the animals were soon replaced by steam locomotives. In the 1840s this railroad was one of the engineering wonders of the world, but by 1855 it had been abandoned as obsolete.

You can reach the first of these hiking trails, which is 1 mile (1.6 km) long, by driving to the Lemon House on US 22, 7 miles west of the junction with US 220. A guide to the numbered posts along this trail can be purchased here for a nominal fee. The house was once the home of Samuel Lemon, who by selling coal and timber to the Portage Railroad and food to workmen and passengers, became one of the richest men in Cambria County.

As you begin walking west from the Lemon House notice the stone ties or sleepers that have been exposed. The fairly deep cuts were made by hand. Unlike wooden ties, the sleepers were unconnected and did not maintain the separation between the rails. Despite their great mass (over 400 pounds) the sleepers moved and settled and derailments were frequent.

Keeping left at the trail junction, you soon pass a stone culvert under the old grade. Notice its keystone arch. How elegant compared with the concrete pipe used to carry the same intermittent stream under the return trail! Next you pass two trails on the left leading to the picnic area and

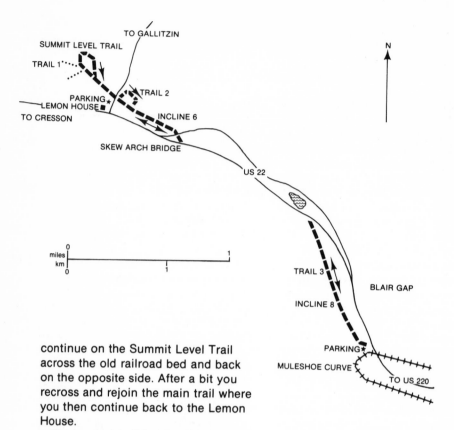

continue on the Summit Level Trail across the old railroad bed and back on the opposite side. After a bit you recross and rejoin the main trail where you then continue back to the Lemon House.

The second trail is 1.3 miles (2.1 km) long. It also begins at the Lemon House, but heads east across the Gallitzen Road, where you pick up the wood-chip path next to the excavated engine house for Incline 6. Bear left on the loop that leads you through a stone quarry where the sandstone sleepers were hand cut without the aid of explosives. This loop leads you back to the incline, where you now bear left past a reconstructed portion.

Note that the primitive design of the portage railroad required two full sets of rails rather than a single set with a bypass halfway down. Along the incline you pass a white oak over two hundred years old. Somehow it es-

caped cutting in the construction of the incline.

Farther downhill you jog left across a side road and a short distance beyond come to the busy westbound lanes of US 22. Use great care in crossing to arrive at the skew arch bridge and the end of this trail. The bridge is the site of a preexisting wagon road that crossed over the portage railroad and continued to carry traffic until 1922. You now retrace your steps to the Lemon House with a climb of only 266 feet (81 meters).

The third part of this hike takes you

up Incline 8 and is 1.7 miles (2.7 km) long. You need your car to reach it. Leaving the Lemon House, turn left on US 22, proceed downhill 2.6 miles, and park on the right just before the new portage railroad bridge, also known as the Muleshoe Curve.

The new portage railroad, built in 1855, was a last gasp attempt to save the canal system. It replaced the entire system of levels and inclines with a conventional railroad, but lasted only two years. In 1857 the state sold the whole system to the Pennsylvania Railroad. This bridge is still used by Conrail.

To reach Incline 8, follow a gated road next to the parking area. After some 200 yards (200 meters), it switches back to the start of Incline 8. With a vertical rise of 308 feet (94 meters) and a grade of six percent, this is the highest and steepest of the ten inclines.

The excavated ruins of Engine House 8 lie at the top of the incline. You continue on this level for another .3 mile (500 meters), but beyond that, it has been obliterated by the eastbound lanes of US 22. Indeed, most of Incline 7 and the level above it also appear to have been destroyed by the modern highway, a pity, given the spectacular nature of Blair Gap between here and Incline 6. Once again, retrace your steps and return to your car.

21 Long Mountain

Total distance: 5 miles (8 km)
Walking time: 3½ hours
Vertical rise: 760 feet (230 meters)

When the Penn State Outing Club first began exploring terrain prior to developing what is now the Mid State Trail back in 1967 or 1968, one of the early efforts covered the part of Long Mountain between US 322 and Stillhouse Hollow. All day a small band of hikers pushed through brush and climbed over rocks and blowdowns. At the end of the day they reported no trail could ever be built across Long Mountain. In 1972 the club returned with three years experience in trail building and the knowledge that sooner or later the Mid State Trail would have to traverse Long Mountain if it was ever to be extended east of US 322. The trail built that year is still rough and rocky but it has repeated views to the south over Coxes Valley and east up the Faust and Greens valleys. The roughest part is the dramatic descent into Stillhouse Hollow where much of it still looks more like a rockslide than a trail, and boulders seem to resist the force of gravity more from sheer habit than from any real means of support. Farther down the mountainside large hemlocks add their rugged grandeur to the setting.

Approach the hike from the Seven Mountains Roadside Rest on US 322 between Milroy and Potters Mills. The rest area is accessible only from the westbound lane. If you are in the eastbound lane, continue past the area for 1.6 miles, turn right at the junction with old US 322 just north of the Laurel Creek Reservoir, swing around

Penn State Outing Club steps

and go left back up US 322.

The rest area's two-hour parking limit has been lifted for day hikers but an overnight parking ban exists. The rest area is closed in winter.

To start, pick up the blue-blazed side trail at the water pump, proceed across the causeway, and enter the woods for the climb up the north flank of Long Mountain. After .3 mile (500 meters) the trail intersects the orange-blazed Mid State Trail. Notice the trail register at this junction.

You turn left along the orange-blazed trail, which soon reaches the ridge, and .6 mile (1 km) farther you have a good view over Coxes Valley to the southeast. The highway noise of US 322 is far enough away for you to hear Laurel Creek 650 feet (200 meters) below. Soon you reach Chickadee Rocks, where there are extensive views of Thick, Strong, and Jacks mountains to the east and south. This site is named for the tiny, hardy birds that inhabit these ridges through the severest winter storms.

After another .3 mile (500 meters) you bypass a blue-blazed trail on the left—you use this to return to the ridge from Stillhouse Hollow. You pass another overlook to the south and the trail becomes rockier as you approach the gap carved through Long Mountain by Lingle Stream. The best overlook is at the edge of this gap. To the left is Faust Valley and Big Poe Mountain. Long Mountain extends east in front of you, while to your right is Greens Valley and the Mid State Trail.

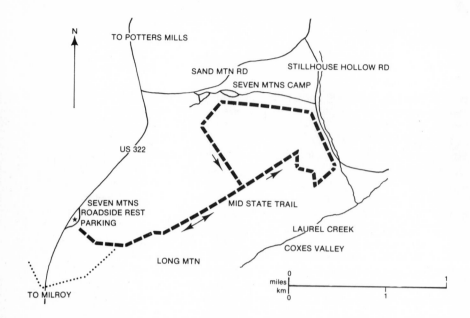

If you wish to shorten your hike by turning back, this is the place to do it. Once you begin the steep descent into Stillhouse Hollow (presumably named because a house with a still existed there) you will find it less exerting to return via the blue-blazed trail from Seven Mountains Scout Camp. About 50 yards (50 meters) from the top you pass Prudential Rock, named by the scouts who helped cut this trail. Your best view of the rock is from below. Toward the bottom the trail switches back past large hemlock trees, which must be very old to have grown to such size on this slope.

At the bottom of the hill the orange-blazed Mid State Trail turns right on the road, but you turn left. After .3 mile (500 meters) look sharply left for a small red pine plantation; just beyond it turn left, uphill, along the white

blazes marking the edge of the state forest land. If you cross a small run on the road you have missed this turn.

The white-blazed trail climbs steeply but then levels off to become a woods road. You eventually see the Seven Mountains Camp buildings and pond on the right, and the road becomes passable to cars. Now look closely for the spot where the road swings away from the white blazes; to your left is the triple blue-blazed start of the trail that leads you back to the ridge.

After following the blue-blazed trail through the woods for a bit, turn left on an old woods road. You soon begin the climb to the junction with the orange-blazed Mid State Trail. Turn right, retrace your steps past Chickadee Rocks, and bear right on the blue-blazed side trail by the register to return to your car.

22 Little Flat

Total distance: 5.9 miles (9.4 km)
Walking time: 3½ hours
Vertical rise: 850 feet (260 meters)

Forest renewal

In the Seven Mountains region of Centre, Huntingdon, and Mifflin counties, near State College, lies an unusual bog known as the Bear Meadows Natural Area. As this region was never glaciated, Bear Meadows is not a northern bog but rather a type usually found in the Southern United States. The meadows are thought to have been created by beavers in a region of poor drainage about 10,000 years ago. Although the pond formed by their dams covered over three hundred acres, it was shallow. Over the intervening millennia it has filled with peat, and microscopic examination of cores taken from the area shows the nature of the ghost forests of the past. Spruce pollen in the bottom layers shows that at the height of the last ice age these ridges were covered with spruce forests, or taiga, such as those found in Siberia and northern Canada today. As the ice retreated, spruce gave way to pine, and it in turn gave way to the richly diverse forests found by the colonists. Many unusual plant species are found in the bog, including carnivorous plants and specimens of red and black spruce as well as clumps of highbush blueberry. You are welcome to explore the meadows but prepare for wet feet and take a compass as it is easy to get "turned around" there. This hike follows much drier trails affording repeated views of the meadows from the surrounding ridges.

The beginning of the trail is 3.7 driving miles from the junction of Bear Meadows Road and US 322 east of Boalsburg. Follow Bear Meadows Road south past Skimont and Galbraith Gap. Turn right at a white-painted barn onto Laurel Run Road and follow it up the northern flank of Tussey Mountain. The road duplicates the route of the Linden Hall Lumber Company's narrow-gauge logging railroad and is therefore narrow, so be sure to honk as you approach each of the three blind curves. The outside loop at the second switchback is reputed to be the sharpest turn on any road in the state.

If no parking space is available when you reach the Mid State Trail crossing (don't block the gate on the Little Shingletown fire road), you can park at Little Flat Fire Tower by driving over the ridge top and following Little Flat Road (if the gate is open) to the left 1.1 miles.

Begin hiking left on the orange-blazed Mid State Trail, proceeding along the exceedingly rocky railroad bed for .3 mile (500 meters) to the end of the last switchback. Swing uphill to the Little Flat Road and bear left. In .2 mile (300 meters) you reach an overlook with views of Bald Knob, Nittany Mountain, and Penn's Valley. Continue on the road past the unmarked junction with the Shingletown Trail to the base of Little Flat Fire Tower. Little Flat is used during the high fire danger periods of April-May and October-November when trees are bare and snow is absent.

On a clear day the tower views are extraordinary. Most of the State College urban area is discreetly concealed

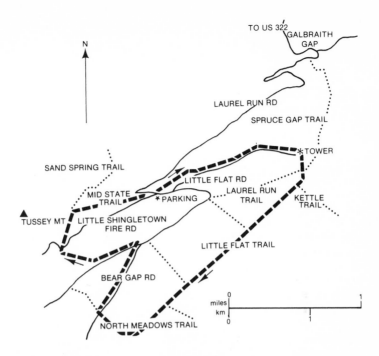

behind Bald Knob but you can see Mount Nittany as well as Tussey Ridge, Thickhead Mountain, and Broad Mountain. To the east Penn's Valley stretches to its end beyond Woodward. The isolated ridge in this valley is Egg Hill.

You now take the Mid State Trail, which here follows the Kettle Trail, south into the woods from the base of Little Flat Tower. Shortly you intersect the Laurel Run and Spruce Gap trails. Spruce Gap is an old name for Galbraith Gap but it is unlikely that spruce grew here. Except in acid bogs, spruce has not grown wild in Pennsylvania for many thousands of years. The many spruce-named gaps, runs, and mountains in Penn's Woods were likely due to mistaking hemlock for spruce.

The Kettle Trail soon breaks off to the left; you continue ahead on the Little Flat Trail another .5 mile (800 meters) to the first overlook of the Bear Meadows region.

Move along the edge of the ridge past a series of overlooks and the white-blazed Fleetfoot and 4-H trails. At the next intersection bear right on the North Meadows Trail along the ridge top, following it downhill to Bear Gap Road, on which you turn right. In another .6 mile (900 meters) turn left at the bottom of the hill onto the Laurel Run Road. Just beyond the Sand Spring hunting camp turn right onto the Sand Spring Trail and cross Laurel Run (you usually can find a log or plank in back of the camp) to bear left on the obvious but unblazed trail. You soon begin climbing the south flank of Tussey Mountain. When you reach the Little Shingletown fire road, jog right a short distance before continuing up Tussey Ridge. You rejoin the Mid State Trail at this jog.

At the top of Tussey Mountain turn right. This section of trail is a delightful walk, and it is a pity it is so short a distance back to the fire road and your car.

23 Little Juniata Water Gap

Total distance: 6 miles (9.7 km)
Walking time: 4½ hours
Vertical rise: 1,300 feet (395 meters)

Water gaps are formed where large streams cut through a layer of hard sandstone as it slowly uplifts on a geologic time scale. The most widely known and best-developed of these gaps is the Delaware Water Gap on the eastern border of the state. Traditionally, these gaps are avenues of communication. They were threaded first by Indian paths, then by wagon roads, canals, and railroads, and finally by the highways of today.

All such water gaps are by their very nature highly scenic, but only four in Penn's Woods have foot trails to scenic vistas. The five major water gaps of the Juniata River and its various branches are particularly undeveloped in this sense. On this hike you reach one of these gaps, the only one in the state without a highway through it.

Unlike most hikes in this book, this one does not loop back to the start. Unless you wish to backtrack, leave one car at the Pennsylvania Fish Commission parking area in the gap itself. To reach it, turn off US 22 on the paved road to Alexandria at the bridge over the Frankstown Branch of the Juniata. In Alexandria turn left just past the factory, go through the village of Barree, cross the one-lane bridge over the Little Juniata, and take the first left to the end of the road. Leave one car here and retrace your route to US 22.

Now turn right and drive .7 mile to Water Street (PA 453), and follow that

View from Tussey Mountain

road to the right for .8 mile. Then turn right on PA 45 and drive 4.6 miles, passing through the village of Spruce Creek, to the Colerain Picnic Area by Spruce Creek Inn and a Mobil station, all on the right. Park near the picnic shelter.

You will not find much water along the trail so fill your canteen at the pump next to the Mid State Trail sign, where you begin. This was the original starting point of the Mid State Trail, but since the recent extension to the Little Juniata Natural Area, the old Mid State here has become a blue-blazed side trail.

Above the park you climb the flank of Tussey Ridge on well-built switchbacks. At .7 mile (1.1 km) you reach Indian Overlook, more than 650 feet (200 meters) above Spruce Creek. This natural overlook permits views far up Nittany Valley and the route of the Penn's Creek Indian Path (now PA 45). The drop-off from the cliff is deceiving, and there have been two fatal falls here in recent years. It is the most dangerous spot on the Mid State Trail, so please be careful.

Continue across a charcoal flat that provided fuel for Colerain Forge, turn left on the Colerain Road, and bear right up the road past the junction with Brady Road. Continue straight on the road where the blue blazes turn right. At 1.9 miles (3 km) you reach the overlook of Spruce Creek Valley and Warriors Mark Run.

Follow the road to the ridge top, and turn sharply right onto the orange-blazed Mid State Trail along the very top of Tussey Ridge. You soon come to repeated overlooks of Round Top Mountain and at 2.8 miles (4.5 km) pass the blue-blazed Rainbow Trail.

As you continue down the ridge the trail becomes rougher. Take time to enjoy repeated views southeast to the village of Petersburg nestled at the foot of Warrior Ridge. If the day is clear you can also see Terrace Mountain, Stone Mountain, and Butler Knob on the horizon. The Loop, a high bend in Tussey Ridge, is visible to the south from some of the overlooks.

Finally, at 4.4 miles (7 km), you reach one of the great overlooks of Central Pennsylvania, where Tussey Mountain falls away into the Little Juniata Natural Area. On a really clear day you see all the way to the south end of Nittany Valley where the Evitts and Tussey ridges touch south of Loysburg. You also see over three different folds of the same ridge to

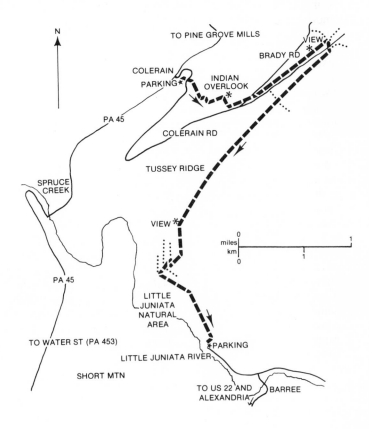

Blue Knob on the horizon and can look right over Short Mountain. The views stretch around to the right over Canoe Mountain and across Nittany Valley to Bald Eagle Ridge and the Allegheny Front.

Bear left and follow the orange blazes down the ridge line. At 4.9 miles (7.9 km) you reach the highest of three quarry levels and another view. Turn sharply left and descend steeply on a funicular grade that connects this level with two more down the mountain. Tuscarora sandstone was quarried here for "ganister," rock used to line iron furnaces, and railroad ballast.

Turn left on the lowest level and follow it past yet another view and two large quarries. It is unclear how the quarried stone reached the railroad since this lowest level is still far above the tracks. Conrail's main east-west line now runs through this gap and trains are frequent. (The trains then pass through tunnels under the northern spur of Short Mountain, just across the gap.)

At 5.3 miles (8.6 km) turn right and descend again along the corner of the ridge. A small cairn about 200 yards (200 meters) down marks a last view through the water gap. From here the remaining descent is uneventful until you swing right off the ridge and through dense woods for the final drop to the parking lot and your car.

24 Greenwood Fire Tower

Total distance: 6.5 miles (10.5 km)
Walking time: 4 hours
Vertical rise: 1,400 feet (425 meters)

A mountain panorama and a glimpse of the early iron industry await you on this hike. Charcoal furnaces, the relics of which you see along here, provided the country with iron from before the Revolution until late in the nineteenth century. The intense industrial activity that existed at this now peaceful location began in 1837, and the site's Greenwood Furnace continued operations until December 1904. It was one of the longest operating charcoal iron furnaces in the country.

Your hike starts and ends at Greenwood Furnace State Park on PA 305, which is 5 miles east of the junction with PA 26 at McAlevys Fort in Stone Valley. You can park in the lot next to park headquarters at the junction of PA 305 and Black Lick Road.

Begin walking down Black Lick Road. Almost immediately a large mound with trees growing from it appears on your right. The large stone structure behind it is the rebuilt replica of Stack 2 at Greenwood Furnace. A recent archeological excavation has revealed the location of Stack 1 off to the side. The siting of these furnaces called for a source of iron ore. The high-grade ore used in the furnace came from the hematite quarries on Brush Ridge west of the park. More importantly, the furnace had to be located in a vast tract of forest that could supply charcoal to smelt the ore. As most level land near here had been cleared for farming, only the steeper mountainsides were still forested.

Replica of Greenwood Furnace Stack 2

Water power was also required to run the air blast.

The production of charcoal was handled by woodsmen and colliers. First the woodsman had to carve a level area called a coal hearth or charcoal flat from the mountainside. You see several of these flats as you go up Broad Mountain. The woodsman also had to make a wagon road from one flat to another so the charcoal could be transported to the iron furnace. You follow such old charcoal roads at several places. Once a new flat was built, the woodsman had to cut, split, and stack all the trees in the vicinity. At this point, the collier took over and covered the stack with earth and/or wet leaves and set it afire. Now came the long and lonely time as the collier tended the fire for ten days to two weeks. If the fire didn't get enough air it expired and had to be rekindled. If it received too much air, the entire stack would burn to worthless ash.

Even when the stack was finally converted to charcoal the collier had to wait until it cooled enough so it would not reignite when it was opened to the air. When the furnace operated, it consumed daily the charcoal from two acres of woodland.

Charcoal operations eventually reached as far as Big Flat and even across Thickhead Mountain down into Bear Meadows. The end did not come from competition with high-grade ore from the Mesabi Range in Minnesota, but from exhaustion of the forests during the first decade of this century.

Continue on Black Lick Road across

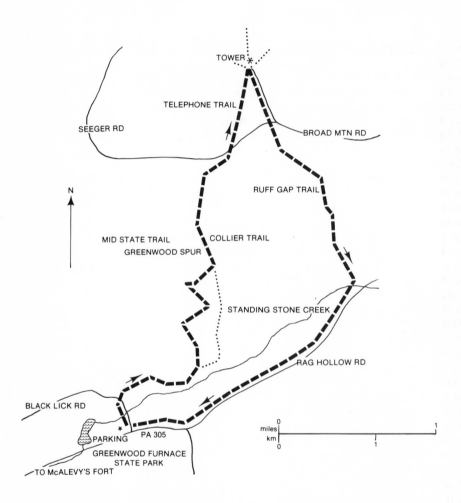

TOWER

TELEPHONE TRAIL

SEEGER RD

BROAD MTN RD

N

RUFF GAP TRAIL

MID STATE TRAIL
GREENWOOD SPUR

COLLIER TRAIL

STANDING STONE CREEK

RAG HOLLOW RD

BLACK LICK RD

PARKING   PA 305

GREENWOOD FURNACE
STATE PARK

TO McALEVY'S FORT

miles
km

0

0

1

1

Standing Stone Creek, past the super-intendent's house, and turn right on the blue-blazed Greenwood Spur of the Mid State Trail. Head across the meadow and into the woods. Here you wander east past more ruins and some very large white pines, then along several old roads, and across a small run. Bear left and begin climbing, shortly crossing a charcoal flat with wild dogwood growing on it. You turn right at the next charcoal flat.

Now begins a steep climb up Broad Mountain on an old charcoal road. At 1.8 miles (2.9 km) the Greenwood Spur turns left on the Collier Trail. By

the time you reach the Seeger Road
the grade has leveled. Follow the
blazes right for some 200 yards (200
meters), and then bear left on the
Telephone Trail to the base of Greenwood Fire Tower.

If the day is clear the views from the
tower are spectacular. To the north is
Indian Wells Overlook above Bear
Meadows and Little Flat Fire Tower
(see Hike 22). Thickhead Mountain
stands with the microwave relay at its
east end. Stone Gap, Grass Mountain,
Slate Ridge, Long Mountain, and the
other Broad Mountain are together,
with upper Stone Valley and Stone
Mountain itself bending off toward the
horizon. Jacks Mountain is the one
with the conspicuous gap to the side
of Milligan's Knob. On a really clear
day you may see several ridges beyond the Juniata.

To return by a different route, leave
the blazes and follow the tower access
road to its junction with the Seeger
and Broad Mountain roads. From here
bear slightly to the right and continue
into the woods on the unmarked but
obvious Ruff Gap Trail. This trail appears to be another old charcoal road
and passes several more flats on its
way down into Rag Hollow. At the
bottom, you pass the Dutch Shanty
hunting camp and continue to Rag
Hollow Road, where you turn right
across Standing Stone Creek and
proceed for 1.4 miles (2.2 km) to PA
305. Bear right on PA 305 past the tree
nursery and .3 mile (500 meters) farther you are at the park office and
your car.

25 Yost Run

Total distance: 7.1 miles (11.4 km)
Walking time: 4¾ hours
Vertical rise: 1,295 feet (395 meters)

A waterfall in the remote depths of Yost Run Canyon is the attraction on this part of the Chuck Keiper Trail. The trail, opened in 1977, is a memorial to Charles F. Keiper, conservationist and sportsman, who was the district game protector in western Clinton County for twenty-two years. The commemoration is a singular tribute to a law enforcement officer.

A regrettable feature of this hike is the large clearcuts resulting from devastation by the oak-leaf roller from 1968 to 1972. This native insect underwent a population explosion and repeatedly defoliated the large stands of oak on the Allegheny Plateau. The oak mortality ranged from fifty percent to one hundred percent over many thousands of acres. The clearcuts on this hike and along PA 144 are salvage cuts designed to save as much timber and pulpwood as possible and to reduce the forest fire hazard resulting from such vast stands of dead trees.

Due to repeated stream crossings this is a trail better hiked when water levels are low. Only one stream crossing is bridged and at the others you must hop on rocks or wade across.

The trailhead for this hike is on PA 144, 13.4 miles northeast from the intersection with PA 879 near Moshannon. You can also reach it by driving 17.2 miles south on PA 144 from the junction with PA 120 in Renovo. There is plenty of parking space in a borrow pit on the northwest side of the high-

Ledges along Yost Run

way, .1 mile south of the Eddy Lick Trail.

You begin by hiking north along the highway to the unblazed but signed Eddy Lick Trail and then turning left. The trail, which here is actually a jeep road that leads to several hunting camps, quickly enters an extensive salvage cut. You move straight across the clearcut, go through a narrow band of trees, and then cross another salvage cut. At 1.4 miles (2.2 km) you reach the Chuck Keiper Trail at Crystal Spring Hunting Camp, 10-C-30. Circle around the camp on the trail and start your descent down the second fork of Yost Run. This trail is marked with yellow blazes of variable sizes and shapes. A double blaze means a turn or stream crossing. The second fork soon begins to cut a spectacular gash of its own, leaving you and the trail high above on the steep, rocky slope. Near the end, the trail switches back down to streamside.

At 2.9 miles (4.6 km) you reach Yost Run and turn upstream, where you begin to encounter the chutes and cascades of this beautiful stream. You cross Yost Run six times and then cross a smaller side stream from Log Hollow on your left. After seven more crossings of the run you make your last one on ancient log bridge. At 5.3 miles (8.5 km) the Kyler Fork comes in on the far side of the run and just beyond you reach the waterfall.

True, the fall's total drop is only 13 feet (4 meters), but even waterfalls of this modest size are rare in unglaciated regions. Presumably, the falls

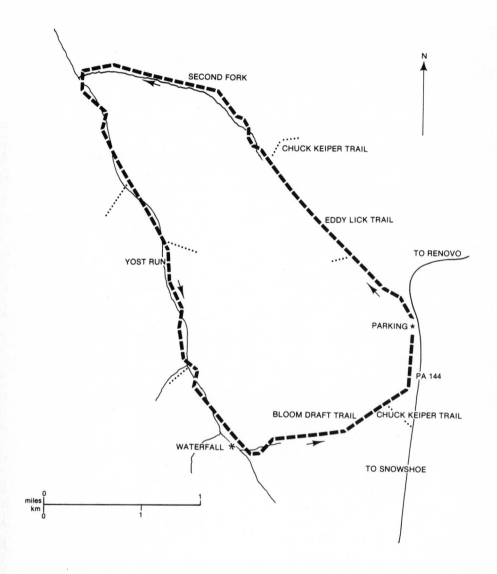

exist due to a layer of unusually resistant rock.

Complete your hike by following the blazes upstream and turning left up Bloom Draft in front of Hunting Camp 10-C-244. Draft in this sense is an archaic but American usage meaning a gulch or canyon. It still occurs in such place names. After you pass Camp Bloom, 10-C-23, you reach a woods road junction, where the Chuck Keiper Trail turns right on a chewed-up haul road. You go straight ahead on an unblazed old woods road that brings you out on PA 144 at 6.7 miles (10.8 km). Turn left along the highway and keep to the left facing traffic for the walk back to your car.

26 Eddy Lick Run

Total distance: 7.4 miles (11.8 km)
Walking time: 4¼ hours
Vertical rise: 950 feet (290 meters)

Old logging railroad grade

Traces of a splash dam and a logging railroad make this hike on the West Loop of the Chuck Keiper Trail an historic trek. A splash dam permitted logging along streams that were too small to float logs even in the spring flood. Most splash dams were temporary affairs made of logs and earth but the one on Eddy Lick Run was built largely of rock and may be the best-preserved in the state.

Toward the end of the nineteenth century the development of steam-powered geared locomotives allowed logging where the streams were too small even for splash dams. Such locomotives were run at the lowest gear in order to provide the greatest power and traction. In this way grades up to fifteen percent could be negotiated with even a couple of log cars. But the price for the feat was the sacrifice of speed; such locomotives were limited to about 15 miles per hour flat out.

By the early part of this century, geared locomotives were being built by three different manufacturers in weights of ten to over a hundred tons. Today a museum at Corry, Pennsylvania, has the only Climax locomotive and the Pennsylvania Lumber Museum at Denton Hill State Park the only Shay locomotive left in the state. You must visit the Cass Scenic Railroad at Cass, West Virginia, if you want to see a geared locomotive in operation.

The trailhead for this hike is on the De Hass Road .2 mile from PA 144. On PA 144 the De Hass Road is 15 miles northeast from the junction with PA

879 near Moshannon or 15.5 miles south from the junction with PA 120 in Renovo. Park where the pipeline crosses the De Hass Road. This hike is best taken during the low water season due to the many stream crossings on Eddy Lick Run.

Start by heading southeast, or right, as you drive in down the pipeline swath toward Dry Run. The swath is evidently used by motorcyles and other off-road vehicles, for you can see evidence of their deleterious effects in the water-soaked soil in Dry Run Hollow.

After picking your way across and around the muddy spots, you climb the next hill through an oak-leaf roller salvage cut. In the second valley you cross Eddy Lick Run for the first time and turn left, downstream, following the yellow blazes of the Chuck Keiper Trail. In places the trail has been cut into the side of the valley, while at others it follows closely along the stream bank. After six crossings of Eddy Lick Run the trail meets and turns left on an old logging railroad grade. You can tell this is an old railroad grade and not a haul or skid road by the uniformity of its grade, its lack of sharp turns, and the frequent and regularly spaced transverse depressions formed where the ties rotted in place.

In about 50 yards (50 meters) the railroad grade crosses a side stream. The bridge is long gone, but some of its old timbers can still be seen in the streambed. Another 200 yards (200 meters) brings you to the old splash

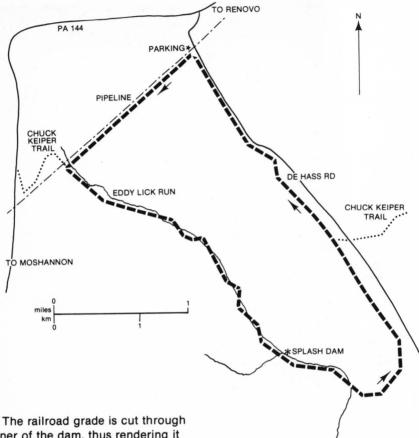

TO RENOVO

PA 144

PARKING *

N

PIPELINE

CHUCK
KEIPER
TRAIL

DE HASS RD

EDDY LICK RUN

CHUCK KEIPER
TRAIL

TO MOSHANNON

0
miles
km
0   1

1

* SPLASH DAM

dam. The railroad grade is cut through a corner of the dam, thus rendering it useless. The spillway is at the far side and a few old timbers still remain. In use, the pond behind the dam was allowed to fill while logs were piled in front of the spillway. All trees and brush were cleared from the valley below so that logs wouldn't hang up on them. When all was ready, the spill-way gate opened and the flood picked up the logs and carried them away. Crews of men ran along both sides of the stream to refloat stranded logs before the splash was over. It was a labor-intensive method of getting logs to a sawmill.

After you investigate the old dam, continue along the trail. About .3 mile (500 meters) along a substantial white pine is growing in the middle of the old railroad grade. It has been a long time since any trains passed this way! In another 200 yards (200 meters) or so, you cross Eddy Lick Run for the last time at the ruins of a railroad bridge. This bridge shows conclusively that the splash dam was not used after the railroad was built. Had a splash full

of logs hit this bridge an awful mess
would have occurred.

Shortly beyond the old bridge site
you bear left and start the long climb
back to the plateau. The white blazes
here mark the boundary of Sproul
State Forest not the trail, so stick with
the yellow blazes. After .2 mile (400
meters) you bear left along a jeep
road. When it curves right you can see
you are on another old railroad grade.
This grade also appears to be standard
gauge so it probably was a spur of the
one back in Eddy Lick Run. Logging
railroads were built in a wide variety of
gauges. The advantage of standard
gauge was that log cars could go
straight onto any regular railroad
and be hauled to a distant sawmill.
However, in early logging operations
narrow gauges and the slow speed of
geared locomotives meant sawmills
had to be close to cutting sites.

At 5.7 miles (9.1 km) the Chuck
Keiper trail turns off the old railroad
grade and quickly turns right on a
jeep road. To reach your car turn left
here and follow the jeep trail for about
275 yards (250 meters) to its end at a
hunting camp. In front of the camp
bear right on the same old railroad
grade. Follow it as it continues its
gentle climb past a small pond and
spring and finally a white pine plantation.

At 6.4 miles (10.3 km) bear left on
the De Hass Road. It is 1 mile (1.6 km)
back to your car at the pipeline. Notice
that the old railroad grade continues
on the far side of De Hass Road but is
heavily overgrown.

27 Hook Natural Area

Total distance: 8 miles (13 km)
Walking time: 5 hours
Vertical rise: 1,220 feet (370 meters)

Log footbridge across Panther Run

The Hook Natural Area in Bald Eagle State Forest is the largest officially designated natural area in the state. Today it is approximately five thousand acres of forest with a few trails used occasionally by hunters, hikers, and fishermen. But during the logging era at the turn of the century the hills were busy with railroads, log slides, trails, and haul roads.

The Hook Natural Area is in Bald Eagle State Forest between PA 192 and PA 45. To reach the start of this hike take LR 59009 north from the Christ United Lutheran Church on PA 45 between Hartleton and Mifflinburg. After driving 3.3 miles on this road, turn left on Diehl Road (T 372) which intersects the old Shingle Road. Bear left again and park near the Mifflinburg reservoir.

(For an alternative start off Jones Mountain Road, drive south on Pine Creek Road from its junction with PA 192 about 1 mile south of R.B. Winter State Park. After crossing the first ridge take Jones Mountain Road, on the left, as far as the junction with the Molasses Gap Trail, park your car, and begin hiking.)

If you park at the reservoir, you begin on the old road just to the left of the last reservoir building. After passing the steel gate progress is slow as you are on an old, rocky railroad grade. On your right the north branch of Buffalo Creek flows through a tunnel in the rhododendron, creating a challenge for fishermen seeking native brook trout. The grade is overgrown in places with rhododendron and hemlock.

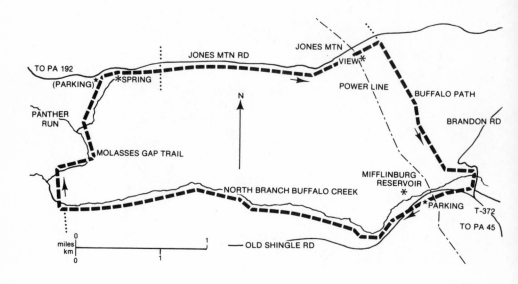

An obscure siding appears on the left at 1.2 miles (2 km) and the Molasses Gap Trail comes down from Little Mountain at 2.7 miles (4.4 km). This trail has been cleared in recent years but the junction to the left of the streambed is still obscure. Continuing on the railroad grade, you soon cross a second and larger streambed coming from between Little and Dogback mountains. Ice Spring is at the left between the two streambeds but it flows only in the wettest times of the year.

In about .2 mile (300 meters) you cross the north branch—on steppingstones in low water or, in high water, on a log about 100 yards (100 meters) downstream. Follow the creek bank until you reach the railroad grade again. When you come to Panther Run cross on steppingstones. (The North Branch has swung off to the west through a virtually impenetrable valley.)

Your last major water crossing appears .1 mile (150 meters) farther. You make this one by going left a way along the stream bank to a grandiose log bridge. Once across the bridge keep to the right bank of Panther Run. You soon pass the Slide Hollow outlet, and after another 100 yards (100 meters) a sign directs you right, toward Jones Mountain Road. The grade is still rocky, and at the point where it becomes covered with brush turn left for Jones Mountain Road ahead.

Head to the right on the road, past an excellent piped spring (here is your last chance to refill your canteen until near the hike's end), and climb gently but steadily for 1.9 miles (3 km) to the power line atop Jones Mountain. Walk south along the power line to the mountain edge for a view of farmlands to the south and Penn's Mountain in the distance. The rise at the far side of the power line swath offers a view of mountains to the west.

To descend Jones Mountain, continue east on the Jones Mountain Road for .2 mile (300 meters) and turn right on Buffalo Path. Legend says this path was a migration route for buffalo moving south from Nippenose Valley. Despite all the mountains, valleys, creeks, and paths labeled "Buffalo" no written records show buffalo existed in the state. Nor has evidence been discovered of buffalo bones or teeth. The buffalo legend seems difficult to substantiate.

The path is fairly straight, although a bit overgrown in places. About .5 mile (900 meters) after you start down Buffalo Path a spring surfaces in the middle of the trail, which disappears and resurfaces as you move down the mountain. Sometimes you can hear it running deep under the rocks.

At the mountain base the slope eases and the path becomes a woods road. Turn left at the intersecting jeep road, cross a stream, and turn right on the intersecting Brandon Road. Bear right at two subsequent intersections and you are soon back at your car. Be aware that camping is not permitted in the Hook Natural Area, as it is the catchment area for a public water supply system.

28 Grass Mountain

Total distance: 8.7 miles (14 km)
Walking time: 5 hours
Vertical rise: 1,530 feet (465 meters)

Historic traces of both the charcoal iron industry and the logging railroad era can be found on Grass Mountain in the Seven Mountains region of Rothrock State Forest. Legends of a lost logging locomotive still haunt Detweiler Valley and the flanks of Thickhead Mountain. From the late 1800s up to 1910 several logging companies cut this region and their tracks were interconnected. Daniel Beidleheimer owned land just to the west of Detweiler Run where he cut prop timber and hauled his logs to Milroy with two Shay locomotives. Every commercially built locomotive had a construction number that was recorded every time the locomotive changed hands and even when it was scrapped, much as for automobiles today. No record has ever come to light that Beidleheimer's Number 2 Shay was ever sold or scrapped. Persistent legends say it is still in the woods, wrecked and covered with rhododendron somewhere on Thickhead Mountain. Since Beidleheimer's land was on the Gettis and Bell ridges, what was his locomotive doing on the other side of the valley on land belonging to Kulp and Thomas or the Reichley Brothers? Was it engaged in pirating his neighbor's timber? If so, that may explain why Beidleheimer couldn't salvage his locomotive after it was wrecked.

The trailhead for this hike is on Stone Creek Road 7 miles west from US 322 at the Laurel Creek Reservoir or 6.7 miles east from PA 26 at Mc-

Upper Stone Valley from Grass Mountain

Alevy's Fort. It can also be reached by driving 10 miles south from US 322 on Bear Meadows Road from a junction east of Boalsburg. Park near the gate on the Long Mountain Trail but don't block it.

The gate marks the start of your long climb up Grass Mountain on the Long Mountain Trail, the boundry of Thickhead Wild Area. Along the way you pass an opening with a good view of upper Stone Valley. A little way beyond the view a charcoal flat lies to the right of the trail. This flat and another farther along show that charcoaling operations for Greenwood Furnace spread far past what is now Alan Seeger Natural Area (see Hike 16).

You reach the top of Grass Mountain at 2.1 miles (3.4 km) and leave Long Mountain Trail behind for the Colon Trail, which enters from the south. As you cross the pipeline swath notice the view of Broad Mountain and Big Kettle to the right. Continue on the Colon Trail across Grass Mountain. You begin a steep descent to Thickhead Mountain Road, which you reach at 3 miles (4.8 km). Bear left for the gradual climb to the south prong of the ridge, now called Thickhead Mountain. The road here follows an old railroad grade and switches back and forth across the narrow ridge before reaching the orange-blazed Shingle Path, part of the Mid State Trail, at 4.2 miles (6.7 km).

Turn left on Shingle Path and descend over rocks to upper Detweiler Valley. The trail turns left along an old

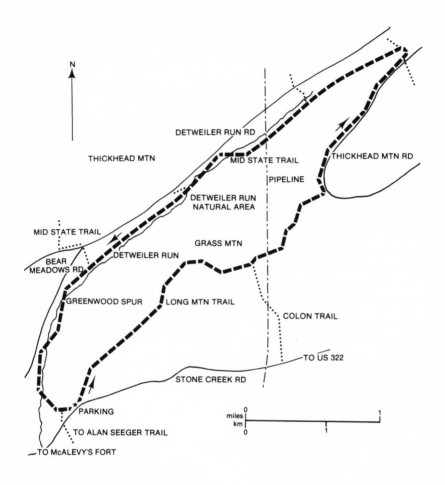

railroad grade laid by the Reichley Brothers Lumber Company of Potters Mills. This ridge-girt valley must have been one of the last tracts in the Seven Mountains to be logged. Legends say the valley was the timber wolf's last refuge in this part of the state. Black bears still inhabit the area but they are shy and your chance of seeing one is small. You may see an old steel rail along this stretch. This evidence of the age of steam shows in its split at one end that the rails were

pulled up with the intent they be used again and not discarded as scrap.

At 5 miles (8.1 km) you pass the Reichley Trail intersection and see a large tulip tree growing in the old railroad grade. Continue along Detweiler Run and cross the pipeline swath. The old railroad grade crosses the run three times, finally ending in a pile of cinders at the junction with the blue-blazed Axe Handle Trail. This part of Detweiler Valley along the Huntingdon–Centre County line was never logged and is now protected as the Detweiler Natural Area. The Kulp-Thomas Company was logging its way up the valley and the border between their land and that of the Reichley Brothers may have been the county line. The law was very strict about timber piracy and if caught, you had to pay three times the value of the timber as punishment. If you didn't have complete and total confidence in your surveyor there was good reason to leave a buffer zone along the borders of your land. So the Detweiler Natural Area and probably a great many other small tracts of virgin timber may really be monuments to poor surveying.

The Mid State Trail continues across a small corner of this forest primeval. After skirting the Detweiler Monument descend the trail along the Kulp-Thomas railroad grade to the point where the Mid State Trail turns right over Thickhead Mountain. Continue ahead on the blue-blazed Greenwood Spur past two more charcoal flats and over Detweiler Run. Just before you reach a hunting camp swing left away from the railroad grade and head east around several other camps. You cross Detweiler Run again, turn left along the rhododendrons, and bear left along the railroad grade. The trail becomes a tunnel through the rhododendrons and crosses the run for the last time.

Where the Greenwood Spur turns right into Alan Seeger Natural Area, you keep straight ahead on the railroad grade for the short distance back to Stone Creek Road and your car.

29 Indian Steps

Total distance: 9.9 miles (16 km)
Walking time: 6 hours
Vertical rise: 800 feet (340 meters)

The Indian Steps seem to be another mystery of Penn's Woods. Nobody today can explain their location (up a mountainside) or say with certainty who built them. According to one legend the steps were built by the Kishacoquillas Indians over three hundred years ago, but Paul Wallace, in his book *Indian Paths of Pennsylvania*, does not even mention them. However, their existence prior to 1911 is documented. The location is unusual because Indian paths usually took easier routes—and an easy route ran across Tussey Mountain less than 3 miles (5 km) away. Called the Standing Stone Path and listed by Wallace (now called PA 26), it passed through a gap between Leading and Rudy ridges just above Monroe Furnace. An Indian on the Standing Stone Path who wanted to use the steps would have had to detour either through Harrys valley or cross over Leading Ridge near its highest part. Indeed, the best preserved steps of all continue up the northwest flank of Leading Ridge and stop, suspiciously, at the boundary of state forest land on the ridge top.

The hike starts and ends at the parking lot on the top of Tussey Ridge on the west side of PA 26, 2 miles uphill from the intersection of PA 45 and PA 26 in Pine Grove Mills. The ridge-top portions of the hike are on the orange-blazed Mid State Trail.

Begin walking south on PA 26 and turn right on the gated road that is the trail at this point. Do not cross PA 26.

Leading Ridge and Stone Valley

Continue past a microwave tower and through the woods to an old clearcut area from the center of which you have a northwest view. Proceed along the trail to the power-line crossing for northwest views of farmland at the foot of Tussy Ridge, heavily wooded Barrens backed by Bald Eagle Mountain, and the Allegheny Front on the horizon. To the southeast you see upper Stone Valley and Stone Mountain on the horizon. At this point the woods road ends, and the Mid State Trail becomes rough and rocky.

You then pass a trail register and another view to the southeast a bit farther. Continuing, you cross the Campbell Trail at 1.4 miles (2.3 km). This trail was a wagon road built across the ridge by a tavern owner named Campbell to deliver thirsty wagoneers to the front door of his tavern and away from the competition in Pine Grove Mills. Proceeding along the ridge, you pass one overlook above Harrys Valley and then three more overlooks.

Finally, 2.9 miles (4.7 km) from PA 26, you reach the top of the Indian Steps, marked by a large pile of stones, or cairn. Turn left and follow the deeply worn path to the edge of the ridge and then down. Many steps are missing but near the ridge top sections are still intact. The Indian Steps Trail continues down to Harrys Valley Road for a steep drop of almost 650 feet (200 meters). For obscure reasons the trail sign here is labeled Crownover Trail.

Turn right on the Harrys Valley

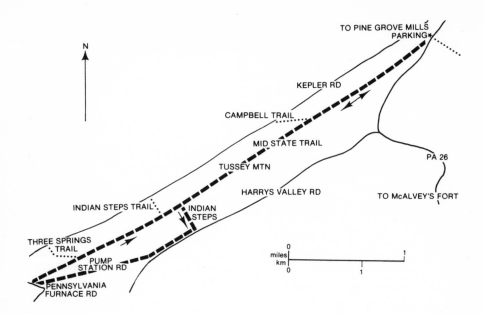

Road. On some weekends the traffic may be heavy but at midweek you may not see a single car in the time it takes to cover the .5 mile (800 meters) on the road. Bear right on the next road, the unmarked Pump Station Road. A couple of springs flowing at, or just above, this junction offer the only water on the hike. The road is normally gated to traffic. Toward the ridge top you pass rocky areas with views of Harrys Valley and Leading Ridge and finally connect with Pennsylvania Furnace Road. Continue ahead past several more view points. To the southeast Jacks Mountain rises over the top of Stone Mountain, and Terrace Mountain comes up from the south and ends abruptly. The Juniata River flows just to the north of the mountain's end and Butler Knob on Jacks Mountain is visible behind Terrace Mountain. One view extends so far south you see Tussey Ridge itself at the loop south of the Little and Frankstown branches of the Juniata, and at one place you can see west over Tussey Mountain to Canoe Mountain.

At the ridge top turn sharply right again on the Mid State Trail and proceed along the gated access road past the site of Tussey Fire Tower. The views from the top were truly spectacular and the hike's other overlooks cannot compare.

Beyond the tower site you enter the woods and pass a southeast view of Stone Valley Lake and a blue-blazed side trail to Kepler Road.

You then begin a fairly long pull of nearly .9 mile (1.4 km) to the Schalls Gap Overlook where a log seat provides a good resting spot. The blue-blazed Indian Steps Trail is .4 mile (600 meters) farther, but only a couple of steps remain on this side of the ridge. For the next .2 mile (300 meters) you follow the old ridge top trail connecting the Indian Steps Trail on opposite sides of the ridge, and then you retrace your steps on the Mid State Trail to return to PA 26 and your car.

30 Black Moshannon State Park

Total distance: 10.7 miles (17.2 km)
Walking time: 5 hours
Vertical rise: 200 feet (60 meters)

Corduroy trail

Black Moshannon State Park, on the Allegheny Plateau in western Centre County, is one of the few parks in the state with a well-developed system of hiking trails. The longest and most interesting of these trails circles a lake, passes through many stands of evergreens, and runs by an active beaver colony. Almost all the trails are suited for ski touring as the plateau's elevation results in a deep and long-lasting snow cover. Surprisingly, this long trek requires little climbing, and much of the hike runs close to the park's feature, a lake formed by the damming of Black Moshannon Creek north of PA 504.

The park is located in Moshannon State Forest at the junction of PA 504 and the Julian Pike. To reach it, drive east on PA 504 from Philipsburg for 8 miles, or west on PA 504 from Unionville for 11.7 miles, or west on the Julian Pike from Julian for 8.4 miles. Park in the beach lot on the north side of PA 504, in the boat-launching lot on the south side, or across the bridge in the lot near the boat rental concession.

The hike starts at the junction of PA 504 and the Julian Pike. Begin by crossing the bridge. Then keep left along the roadside past the boat rental area and at the Westside Road–PA 504 junction bear left up the slope. Pass cabin P6 on your left, then a drinking fountain, and at the cabin area's far side bear to the right for a short distance on the paved road. Then turn left on Seneca Trail, go about .2 mile (350 meters) and jog briefly to the left

on the Hay Road Trail. Continue to the junction with Indian Trail, turn left, and follow it through a planting of jack pine and Norway spruce as far as the Moss Hanna Trail.

Up to this point the trails have been signed but not blazed. The Moss Hanna Trail, which you follow for the next 7.8 miles (12.5 km), is marked with triangular white blazes that vary in size and point in the direction the trail turns. Along the first stretch, the Moss Hanna Trail crosses the head of a long, swampy arm of the lake and on higher ground passes several old beaver dams. Although the trail here is scarcely .6 mile (1 km) from an access road to the local airport, it seems remote as it winds through open woods and dense stands of red pine and Norway spruce, traversing both high ground and the lake's marshy extensions. About 2.8 miles (4.5 km) from the start of the hike, the trail meets the YCC trail, a short loop not included in this hike.

The Moss Hanna Trail now bears left along the fence enclosing Black Moshannon Airport. (The fence and cattle gate on the access road keep deer off the runways.) The trail veers from the fence, circles the end of a runway and passes between the approach lights. You can see Rattlesnake Mountain down the approach light swath.

You now leave the woods and take a corduroy trail across a broad, marshy area, in the midst of which you cross Black Moshannon Creek on a small bridge. In the late summer the creek may be almost dry but in midwinter it

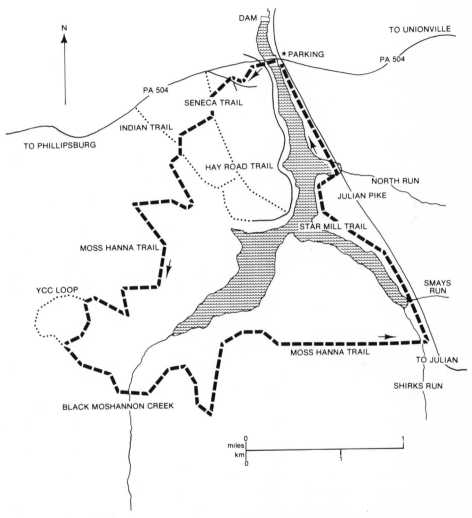

N

DAM

TO UNIONVILLE

★ PARKING

PA 504

PA 504

SENECA TRAIL

INDIAN TRAIL

TO PHILLIPSBURG

HAY ROAD TRAIL

NORTH RUN

JULIAN PIKE

STAR MILL TRAIL

MOSS HANNA TRAIL

YCC LOOP

SMAYS RUN

MOSS HANNA TRAIL

TO JULIAN

BLACK MOSHANNON CREEK

SHIRKS RUN

miles
km

0   1

0   1

flows deep and clear, and rarely freezes. Once across the bridge you climb into the woods, bear left, then right and follow a faint woods road across higher ground to another marshy indenture of the lake.

Here the trail bears right and the woods road becomes clearer. You cross what seems to be a small strip mine and can see pulverized coal on the path and small piles of coal in the brush. Nobody seems to know who operated this mine or when, but the fact is the whole park sits on a sub-surface coal seam. The state does not own the mineral rights and one would guess the owners will someday insist on removing their coal. The lake contains a quantity of acid already and such activity would probably increase its acidity and destroy its ability to support any form of aquatic life.

You soon bear left off the woods road and round the head of the bay via a log bridge over a small stream. Bear left and pass a large spring. Soon you see old beaver dams on the left, an active dam further ahead, and a classic beaver lodge in the pond. Many trees in this area have been felled by the beavers.

The trail then bears east, gradually draws away from the lake, passes through a dense stand of hemlocks, and crosses higher ground before entering another pine plantation. You take another corduroy trail through the marsh along Shirks Run, cross the run on a bridge, and bear left in the trees. The Julian Pike is visible to the right. When you reach it, turn left and walk single file on the left side, facing traffic. After crossing Smays Run, take a sharp left onto unblazed Star Mill Trail and follow it along the lake edge. After .6 mile (1 km) bear left on the road at the first cottage and return to the Julian Pike. Turn left and cross North Run. Once across, walk on the grass to the left of the road. After you pass the road to the group camping area, bear left and finish your hike by traversing the extended picnic area between the road and the lake. You are now at the boat-launching area and close to your car.

North District

31 Gillespie Point

Total distance: 2 miles (3.2 km)
Walking time: 1½ hours
Vertical rise: 900 feet (275 meters)

High above the village of Blackwell at the confluence of Pine and Babb Creeks is a hill called Gillespie Point. It is known locally as Pennsylvania's Matterhorn. The Bureau of Forestry recently cut and blazed a trail to the summit of this hill and sites have been cleared to provide views. The pyramidal shape of Gillespie Point is unusual among mountains in the Allegheny Plateau, and you can see the hill's distinctive pointed outline from as far down Pine Creek as Gas Line Ridge below State Run.

Blackwell marks the southern end of Pine Creek's narrow valley, referred to as the Grand Canyon of Pennsylvania. However, Pine Creek Gorge continues all the way down to the west branch of the Susquehanna near the town of Jersey Shore.

The trailhead is at the junction of PA 414 and Big Run Road in the village of Blackwell. No real parking area exists so park as best you can along the sides of Big Run Road or PA 414.

You begin the blue-blazed trail about 100 yards (100 meters) from the highway at the bend in Big Run Road, following an old wagon road that slabs up the steep side of the gorge. The grade is relentless so move slowly.

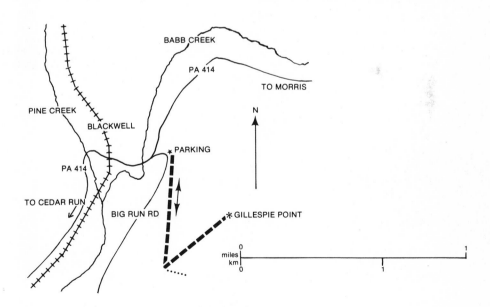

Pine Creek at Blackwell

(You can climb faster this way than if you surge ahead and stop to catch your breath.)

Part way up you pass a walled spring and an extensive stand of white birch. At .6 mile (900 meters) the old wagon road tops out at the edge of the canyon and you turn sharply left to continue up the ridge line. After another .4 mile (700 meters) you enter the clearing around the rock outcrops at the summit. It's an old story in Penn's Woods that you can't see the forest for the trees. If these vistas had not been cut you would have no views during the months the trees were in leaf.

As you pause for breath you look out over a few buildings in Blackwell and the road bridge over Pine Creek. You can't see very far up the creek but you do see an expanse of it downstream to the southwest. The Grand Canyon of Pine Creek, from Ansonia to Blackwell, is a favorite float trip for rafts and canoes. Notice the takeout point just below the bridge. If you walk a few steps through the trees you come to another overlook, with a vista up Babb Creek. You can see a few buildings in Morris far up the valley.

As you return to the first overlook imagine what Pine Creek looked like at the peak of the last continental ice sheet. The ice advanced approximately to the New York State line and Pine Creek carried all the melt water from a vast stretch of the ice front. No wonder its valley looks a bit oversized for the modest stream of today!

You now retrace your steps and return to your car.

32 Pitch Pine Loop

Total distance: 2.5 miles (4 km)
Walking time: 1¼ hours
Vertical rise: 60 feet (20 meters)

Along the Pitch Pine Trail

Pitch Pine Loop is one of many trails blazed primarily for ski touring in recent years. Tiadaghton State Forest, in which this hike is located, has probably undergone the most activity of all twenty state forest districts regarding the clearing and marking of trails for hiking and ski touring. Tiadaghton is an Indian word meaning river of pines, and most of Pine Creek Gorge is located in this state forest. Tioga State Forest to the north contains the balance.

PA 44, the only access to this hike, follows much of the early nineteenth-century Jersey Shore-to-Coudersport Turnpike. This pike was famous for the long distance it traversed through a wilderness devoid of human settlement. Even today, over one hundred fifty years later, PA 44 is virtually bereft of permanent human inhabitants from Haneyville to Sweden Valley. Most of the buildings you see along the way are hunting camps and they are usually occupied only the night before deer season opens.

The trailhead is on the east side of PA 44, 2.6 miles north of the junction

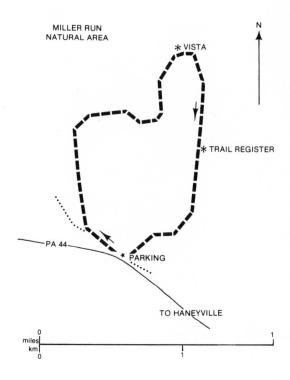

with PA 664 in Haneyville. Park on the small, hard-surfaced area and begin hiking on the blue-blazed trail close by. Bear left, heading slowly away from the highway, and pass behind a hunting camp. (If you don't pass in back of this camp you are following blazes in the wrong direction.) About .3 mile (500 meters) from the start a faint unblazed trail diverges left down a draw into the Miller Run Natural Area. You stay up on the plateau and pass through a stand of scrub oak and the pitch pines for which the trail is named. Both these trees grow on poor, dry, sandy soils. The pitch pine has a superficial resemblance to the red pine on the nearby Baldwin Point hike (Hike 39). Here in Penn's Woods, pitch pines become real forest trees. Before the Revolution, tar and turpentine were made from them, and the rot-resistant wood was used in making water wheels. Look for the characteristic tufts of needles that emerge on miniature branches from the pitch pine's trunk. These tufts help you to distinguish it from red pine.

At 1.4 miles (2.3 km) from the start you reach an overlook with an extensive vista over the 4,000-acre Miller Run Natural Area. The farthest hillsides are on the east side of Pine Creek.

The trail back to the parking area takes off just behind this view. It is not as wide as the old road you followed up, and it twists and turns more through the woods.

You reach a trail register at 2 miles (3.3 km). Please sign in (notice how far people have come to ski and hike here). The last stretch goes by all too fast, but just 100 yards (100 meters) from the end you encounter one more point of interest when you pass through a small stand of tamaracks. Tamaracks are usually restricted to bogs and swamps, but these specimens are growing here on the plateau where it is usually quite dry. The tamarack is a deciduous conifer. Its needles turn a smoky gold color before they are shed in the fall. You now walk the short distance back to the highway and your car.

33 Sizerville Nature Trail

Total distance: 3.2 miles (5.1 km)
Walking time: 2 hours
Vertical rise: 650 feet (200 meters)

Most nature trails are no more satisfying than a walk around the block. The Sizerville Nature Trail is different and makes a good hike. It shows the impact of management practices on the forest and identifies points of interest along the trail. Instead of numbered posts requiring a frequently unavailable interpretive pamphlet, the trail has small information signs at each station. Their life expectancy is only a couple of years but some may escape vandalism for longer periods.

The trailhead is on the west side of PA 155, 1 mile north of the main entrance to Sizerville State Park. Plenty of off-road parking lies behind the large wooden sign. The state park camping area is directly across the highway from the trailhead. The circuit route may be hiked in either direction. A counter-clockwise direction is described here so that you are climbing when you come to an obscure turn near the top of Arnold Hollow. Moving more slowly, you are less likely to miss it.

To begin, turn right, follow the footway some 150 yards (150 meters), bear left to climb another grade, and at .2 mile (300 meters) turn left again for the serious climb up Arnold Hollow. You see by the trail signs this northern hardwood forest consists of beech, sugar maple, yellow birch, and black cherry. Here along the hollow the soil is moist, favoring these species. Arnold Hollow was selectively cut back in 1960, and the better trees, left to

White birches

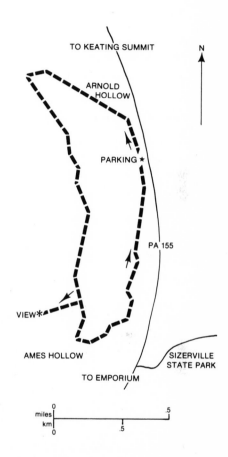

mature, were marked with paint. Some of these paint spots are still visible but they do *not* mark the trail.

Toward the top of the hollow you swing left and find the trail edged with small logs. The footway is very faint in places and a single blowdown can obscure it. You now head south along some large white pines at the ridge edge. The trees must have been very small when the pines were logged here in the 1890s.

As you walk along this and most of the state's other trails during the summer, listen for the towhee. Its call says "drink your tea," with the "tea" trilled. It has a couple of other calls but this is the easiest one to recognize. You'll hear at least ten towhees for every one you see. A common bird the size of a robin, it is also called the woods robin and scratches its living on the forest floor. Half the "large animals" you hear rustling in the brush are towhees. The other half are chipmunks.

At 1.3 miles (2.1 km) you reach the grassy logging road you follow for the remainder of the hike. At 1.8 miles (2.9 km) you arrive at the head of Ames Hollow and the side trail to Bucktail Vista, with its view down the Portage Branch of Sinnemahoning Creek. In Indian times the head of canoe navigation was at Emporium, to the south. From there one carried supplies up the Portage Branch and over Keating Summit to Canoe Place on the Allegheny River.

Back on the trail, you descend past an area clearcut about 1970 that seems to be revegetating very well. Outsized deer herds may prevent clearcuts from rapidly revegetating to trees. You now swing around the south-facing slope of the hill, which is drier than the one you came up and, as a result, has a lot more oaks. Notice the water bars built into the logging road. These helped prevent erosion and also drained wet spots so heavy equipment wouldn't bog down. You now travel rapidly downhill and are soon back at the highway and the end of your hike.

34 Beech Bottom Hemlocks

Total distance: 4.2 miles (6.8 km)
Walking time: 2½ hours
Vertical rise: 900 feet (275 meters)

Footbridge across Hammersley Fork

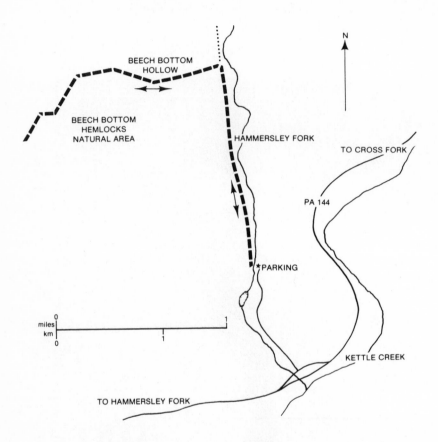

At the head of Beech Bottom Hollow on the Hammersley Fork is a small stand of old growth hemlock, the heart of the 1,500-acre Beech Bottom Hemlocks Natural Area. This stand appears to have been on the border between two logging operations, one headed by a man named Munson and the other headed by the Goodyear brothers. Like similar boundaries, it was not well delineated and to avoid paying triple damages for boundary violation, the operators never cut these trees. The trees are a monument to poor surveying, just like many other small tracts of virgin timber throughout Penn's Woods.

The trailhead is just off PA 144 between the villages of Cross Fork and Hammersley Fork. Over the years the latter village has moved downstream and is now centered about Trout Run. Drive northeast on PA 144 for 1.6 miles from the junction with Kettle Creek Road and then bear left on the old road for .1 mile. Turn left onto a gravel road immediately after crossing the old bridge over Hammersley Fork and in .6 mile more you are at the edge of state forest lands. Park somewhere in the next .1 mile, before you reach the ford across Hammersley Fork. Four-wheel drive and other jeep-type vehicles can negotiate the ford but it is imprudent to attempt the crossing in an ordinary car. Begin by crossing Hammersley Fork on foot. A footbridge about 100 yards (100 meters) upstream is in a dangerous state of disrepair. In low water you can hop across the stream on rocks but in slightly higher water you had best take off your boots and wade. A hiking stick is useful in fording streams.

On the far side turn right on the jeep road along the edge of the stream and eventually swing left toward the valley's west side. The careful observer should see the remains of old hunting camps and railroad grades along the stream valley's bottom.

At 1 mile (1.7 km) you reach the signed junction with Beech Bottom Trail. Should this sign be missing the junction is the first trail you reach by the Hammersley Fork beyond a stone chimney. Turn left and immediately start the long but steady climb up Beech Bottom Hollow. You stick close to the run at first but gradually climb above it. A good spring is just to the left of the trail at 1.9 miles (3 km).

You reach the hemlocks at 2.1 miles (3.4 km), at just about the top of the hollow. A trail register stands to the left. This is the only remaining tract of Pennsylvania's Black Forest, which stretched east of here to Pine Creek and also covered most of Potter County. With the exhaustion of white pine late in the nineteenth century, the price of hemlock rose sharply. The vast stands of hemlock lasted so short a time after the increase that in only three decades they were gone. Entire towns and railroad networks were built to exploit the hemlock, and when it was gone, they too, vanished. But this is what it was like—hemlocks so thick and large that sunlight rarely reached the ground even at midday.

When you have seen enough, retrace your steps to your car.

35

Summerson Run and Owl Hollow

Total distance: 4.4 miles (7.1 km)
Walking time: 2¾ hours
Vertical rise: 1,020 feet (310 meters)

This pleasant walk in the woods is an introduction to the Donut Hole Trail and its many blazed side trails. The trail is located in Sproul State Forest, named after a former governor of Pennsylvania. At nearly 274,000 acres, Sproul is the largest of the twenty forest districts in the state. It is thought to have over 550 miles (900 km) of foot trails, but only about some twenty percent have been blazed or cleared since the Civilian Conservation Corps marched off to World War II in December 1941.

This hike starts on Kettle Creek Road 6 miles upstream from Westport, which is on PA 120. Various maps designate this road as T-308 or LR 18003, but as I could find no signs with either number they are of little use. Just make sure that in Westport you turn on the road immediately to the east of the one-lane bridge over Kettle Creek. Park in the Kettle Creek State Park lot on the east side of the road 6 miles north of PA 120 and 9 miles south of PA 144.

Start by walking southeast along the Kettle Creek Road for .4 mile (700 meters). Keep to the left, facing traffic, and ignore the red blazes of the Donut Hole Trail, which soon cuts through the camping area between the road and creek. At Owl Hollow turn left and follow the blue blazes uphill. The stone structure here appears to be an incinerator from the days of the Civilian Conservation Corps when air quality standards were not a concern.

Huling Ridge Trail

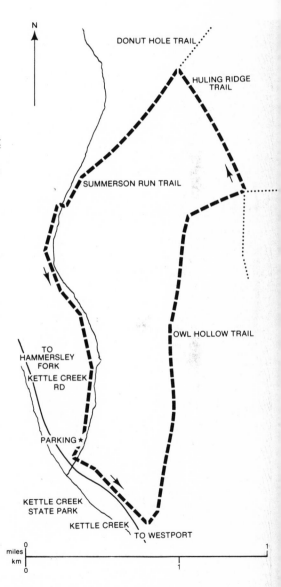

The trail in Owl Hollow keeps to the left of the stream and new footway has been cut in places. The stream flows on the surface only intermittently in summer. Up to your left notice large blocks of sandstone sliding at a geologic pace to the bottom of the hollow.

Towards the top of the hollow you swing right to a junction with the Huling Ridge Trail at 2 miles (3.2 km). This trail is blue-blazed in both directions. Turn left and continue the gentle climb to the red-blazed Donut Hole Trail at 2.5 miles (4.1 km). The many dead trees here are caused by the oak-leaf roller. The damage has resulted in a rather open forest and an acceleration of plant growth on the forest floor, particularly mountain laurel and ferns.

Turn left on the Donut Hole Trail and soon start your descent. At 3.2 miles (5.2 km) Summerson Run comes in from your right. A very pretty little stream, it here flows among large sandstone boulders. At 3.4 miles (5.5 km) you cross the stream, which in low water may flow underground at this point. From here on the trail is cut into the side of the hollow and at times is far above the stream. Summerson Run forms a series of pools and cascades. The larger pools are alleged to harbor native trout.

At 4.4 miles (7.1 km) you reach the parking lot on Kettle Creek Road.

36 Loyalsock Trail

Total distance: 6.3 miles (10.1 km)
Walking time: 4½ hours
Vertical rise: 1,165 feet (355 meters)

View from the Allegheny Front

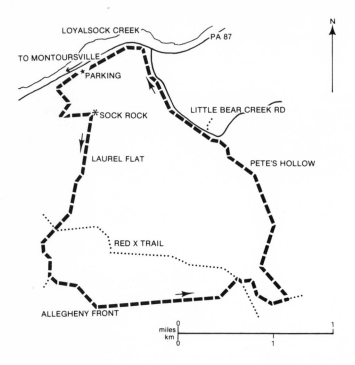

This rugged hike is on one of the oldest maintained trails in central Pennsylvania. The Loyalsock Trail was first marked in 1953 and ten years later was extended and extensively relocated. It parallels Loyalsock Creek, which cuts a deep canyon into the Allegheny Plateau. In contrast with paint-blazed trails, the Loyalsock is marked with tin can lids and round plastic discs nailed to trees—a system modeled on the Northville-to-Lake Placid Trail in the Adirondack Forest Preserve. The red lids and discs bear the yellow letters "LT."

To reach the trailhead drive north 8.9 miles on PA 87 from the junction with US 220 near Montoursville. Several parking spaces are on the east side of the highway.

You immediately begin climbing away from the road and soon bear right on an old road for about 250 yards (250 meters). Then turn left and make a steep climb through a break in the cliffs. Above the cliffs the climb eases off. Hikers have worn a footway into the hillside here but higher up the rocks become larger and you must watch the markers carefully.

At .6 mile (1 km) you pass a large sandstone boulder named Sock Rock and in another 200 yards (200 meters) you are at the top. Laurel Flat, the plateau, is covered with mountain laurel, usually in full bloom about mid-June.

At 1.6 miles (2.5 km) you reach a junction of woods roads. The road to the left is marked with a red X and rejoins the Loyalsock Trail near the head of Pete's Hollow. Continue on the other road across two small streams and then follow the trail left at a fork and left again when it leaves the road. You climb over more rocks and arrive on the Allegheny Front at 2.2 miles (3.6 km).

Despite the prominence of the Allegheny Front in Pennsylvania geography, few places offer a walk along this dividing line. This is one, and as you trek the next 1.2 miles (2 km) the ridge and valley region lies on your right and the Allegheny Plateau on your left. Succeeding overlooks offer views of the North White Deer Ridge with the West Branch of the Susquehanna just east of where the ridge fades.

If you hike in June you may see a show put on by a hen grouse. While her chicks fly or scurry in one direction, she displays her tail feathers and runs across the trail, cheeping piteously, with one wing dragging as if broken. You are expected to fall for this age-old ruse and follow her into the woods. The "broken wing" mends miraculously, and the hen takes flight to circle around and gather her brood.

At 3.5 miles (5.6 km) turn right on a woods road and pass the red X Trail on your left. Turn left at the next junction and at 3.7 miles (6. km) turn left again to head down Pete's Hollow. A short way along a clearcut on your right offers a view of Smiths Knob across Little Bear Creek Valley. The trail down Pete's Hollow is rough and rocky so move carefully. Toward the bottom you pick up an old road grade called Peter's Path, pass a trail register at 4.9 miles (7.9 km), cross Little Bear Creek, and then turn left on the forest road. In 100 yards (100 meters) Loyalsock Trail turns right and starts its climb over Smiths Knob, but you continue ahead and at 5.8 miles (9.3 km) turn left on PA 87 for the short walk back to your car.

37 Boon Road Trail

Total distance: 6.6 miles (10.6 km)
Walking time: 4 hours
Vertical rise: 1,260 feet (385 meters)

Even though Boon Road is "Boone" road on the trailhead sign and all maps, it appears to have no connection with native son Daniel Boone, or any other Boone. Rather, this historic route owes its existence to a little-known military expedition of the Revolutionary War.

In the summer of 1779 Colonel Daniel Brodhead, supporting General John Sullivan's move against the Iroquois, led a force of six hundred men east along what is now the New York–Pennsylvania line. Sullivan defeated the Indians before Brodhead arrived and Brodhead was ordered south to Antes Fort, near the modern-day town of Jersey Shore on the West Branch of the Susquehanna. Brodhead cut a supply road south through what are now Potter and Clinton counties. The road marked the eastern boundary of a refuge for nonfighting Indians, and any Indian who ventured east of it had a price on his head. The refuge was considered a boon to the Indians and Brodhead's road was thus dubbed Boon Road.

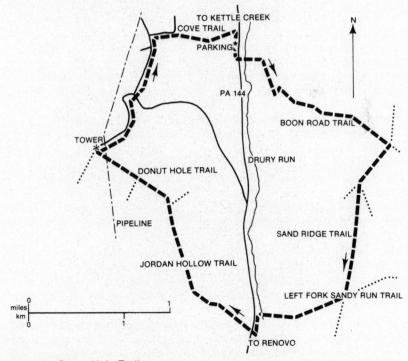

White birch on the Donut Hole Trail

The road fell into disuse and when the Jersey Shore-to-Coudersport Turnpike was built early in the nineteenth century it was routed well to the east of Boon Road. Early settlers along Kettle Creek used Boon Road as a foot trail to bring supplies from Renovo. Today the larger part of the road is a state forest road but over 1.2 miles (2 km) is trail, and this hike combines it with adjoining parts of the Donut Hole Trail in a circuit hike.

The trailhead is on PA 144, 7.1 miles north of PA 120 and 4.7 miles south of Kettle Creek. Park at the Cove Trail on the road's west side.

The first part of the trail is obscure so follow directions closely. Begin walking south along PA 144 toward the Boon Road Trail sign. About 15 yards (14 meters) north of the sign, head straight into the woods via the steep bank. Cross Drury Run and continue on the same straight line through a small bog. About 50 yards (50 meters) from the run you should find yourself on a faint footway along a swath through the trees. If you are not on this swath, zigzag back and forth until you find it. At 300 yards (270 meters) from PA 144 turn right on an old woods road—this is Boon Road and north of here it lies on private land. At this point you have accomplished the hike's most difficult routing.

Swing along the road and begin climbing Boon Mountain on two switchbacks. The trail, occasionally overgrown with scrub oak and mountain laurel, is straight and easy to pick up when you detour around frequent blowdowns. Atop the hill you dip into a hollow that has water, and then move deeper into the usually dry Pong Hollow.

At 1.3 miles (2.1 km) you leave the Boon Road trail, which continues to the Boon Forestry Road, and turn right on the red-blazed Donut Hole Trail. You soon cross Pong Hollow Trail and at 2.4 miles (3.8 km) turn right on the Left Fork Sandy Run Trail to move through a small stand of white birch and cross Drury Run on a log bridge.

Climb the bank and turn left along PA 144 for a short way to the Jordan Hollow Trail and an excellent piped spring. The climb up the hollow is easy, but steady. At 4.3 miles (6.9 km) you pass the Tub Hollow Trail on the right, then the Drury Ridge Trail on the left, and farther along a pipeline swath and an old road. Continue ahead through the spruce trees to Tamarack Fire Tower where, if weather permits, a tower view gives sightings of Kettle Creek Valley to the north and west and West Branch Canyon to the south. A well stands in the clearing around the tower—an unexpected feature atop such a hill.

To continue, backtrack through the spruces, turn left to the end of the tower access road, and follow it across the pipeline into a clearcut. At 5.5 miles (8.9 km), in the middle of the clearcut, turn left on a second road and follow it to another road, where you turn right. After .3 mile (400 meters) bear right on a grassy old road, the Cove Trail, for the brief walk downhill to your car.

38 West Rim Trail

Total distance: 7.4 miles (12.0 km)
Walking time: 4¼ hours
Vertical rise: 600 feet (185 meters)

Measuring distance on the West Rim Trail

The northernmost part of Pine Creek Gorge, long a favorite with white-water canoeists, offers hikers a breathtaking trail along the very edge of Pennsylvania's Grand Canyon. The Grand Canyon was created during the Ice Age when the continental ice sheet blocked drainage to the north. All the melt water from a somewhat triangular portion of North America stretching far into Canada went through this gorge. As you see the tiny stream of today try and imagine it then, its waters white with rock flour.

The hike described here requires a car shuttle. To reach the trailhead turn south off US 6 at Ansonia and follow Colton Road past Colton Point State Park. At 6.5 miles from US 6 turn left onto Painter Road and at 8.3 miles turn left again onto Leetonia Road. Leave one car at the West Rim Trail's northern point at the end of a switchback 9.1 miles from US 6. Then continue south on Leetonia Road to 14.4 miles, turn left onto West Rim Road and drive to the Bradley Wales Picnic Area, where you park.

Pick up the orange-blazed trail at the woods on your right. At the edge of the canyon turn sharply left and move past a succession of views up, down, and across the gorge. Down the canyon, at the mouth of a hollow on the far side, you see a couple of cottages, the remains of the ghost town of Tiadaghton. In logging days it was a sizable town, with a sawmill and logging railroads spread far and wide.

At .6 mile (900 meters), bear left away from the edge to head a nameless side stream and valley. This maneuver begins a trail pattern similar to that of the Tonto Trail in Arizona's Grand Canyon. If the side stream is small a modest excursion is required to move around it; with a large stream the detour may be protracted.

After heading around this first side canyon, return briefly to the canyon's edge before swinging up Ice Break Run, which you cross at 1.4 miles (2.2 km). Follow the trail back to the edge and at 1.9 miles (3 km) bear right on the Ice Break Trail up the side of Little Slate Run. This side canyon is the largest you encounter and offers a view across Little Slate.

At 2.8 miles (4.5 km) bear right off the old road, cross Little Slate Run and turn downstream on the far side past a blue-blazed side trail to Leetonia Road. You quickly pick up another old grade and climb to a side stream of Little Slate Run. Until now you've had good paths, but beyond this point the footway is intermittent and requires a sharp eye for blazes. At 3.8 miles (6.1 km) you are back at the edge to pass a view, cross Tumbling Run, and encounter another view. Many of these views would be enormously improved with the cutting of a few trees.

Horse Run requires only a modest detour but the crossing requires a sharp descent and then a steep scramble upward. By 5 miles (8 km) you are back at the edge, with a clear footway again. At 5.5 miles (8.8 km) you jog left on a woods road and cross Burdic Run. The blue-blazed road continues

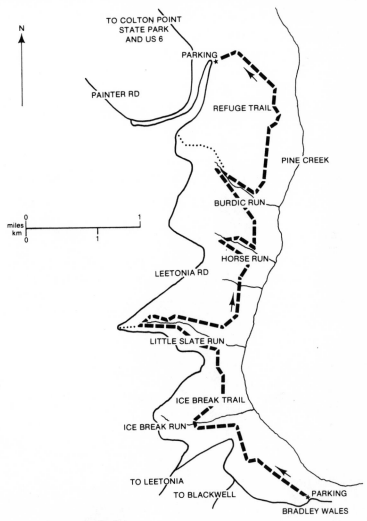

N

TO COLTON POINT
STATE PARK
AND US 6

PARKING

PAINTER RD

REFUGE TRAIL

PINE CREEK

BURDIC RUN

0   1
miles
km
0   1

HORSE RUN

LEETONIA RD

LITTLE SLATE RUN

ICE BREAK TRAIL

ICE BREAK RUN

TO LEETONIA

TO BLACKWELL

PARKING
BRADLEY WALES

left and leads out to Leetonia Road.

Watch the blazes carefully on the far side of Burdic Run as the trail climbs the bank and bears right to an old grade which returns to the run farther downstream. At 5.7 miles (9.1 km) turn left on the Refuge Trail. This trail, like others of the same name around the state, marked a game refuge boundary. Such refuges were common but most have now been abandoned. They were usually established in blissful ignorance of the size and diversity of land required for the home range of the animals they were to protect.

After a short climb the Refuge Trail levels to an old railroad grade. Again, a little judicious cutting would improve the views. Follow this trail up Four Mile Run to the switchback on Leetonia Road and your car.

39 Baldwin Point

Total Distance: 7.7 miles (12.4 km)
Walking time: 4½ hours
Vertical rise: 820 feet (250 meters)

Porcupine scaling a tree

Highlights of this hike are views of the Baldwin Branch of Young Womans Creek and Naval Run, a tributary of Pine Creek, plus a trek on a portion of the Black Forest Trail. Laid out with consummate skill by members of the Bureau of Forestry, the Black Forest Trail is esthetically pleasing and extraordinarily scenic.

The name Black Forest was given to this region west of Pine Creek because its original evergreen forest resembled the Schwarzwald in southern Germany. The virgin stands of hemlock and red and white pine were so dense that sunlight did not reach the forest floor even at midday. The pines were the first to go. They were logged and floated down Pine Creek to the mills in Williamsport. When logging railroads

were built here in the 1890s only the hemlock and scattered hardwoods were left.

Although the Black Forest Trail was completed in 1971, it is already experiencing problems of heavy use. Most arise from backpacking, so only day hikes using the trail are included in this book.

To reach the trailhead drive 11.1 miles north on PA 44 from the junction with PA 664 in Haneyville. Turn left on the Benson Road and drive .5 mile more to the junction with the Dry Run Road. Some off-road parking space has been cleared here.

The trailhead is signed but the first section of the trail heading north is unblazed. However, after only .2 mile (300 meters) you pick up the blue dot

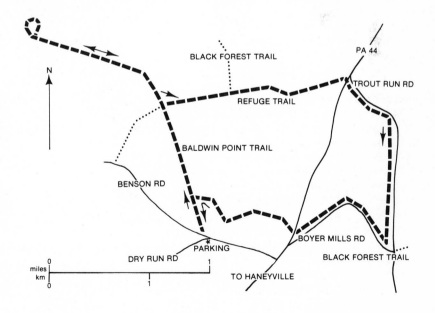

blazes where they come in from the right. Follow the blazed trail ahead past the junction with the signed but unblazed Refuge Trail at .9 mile (1.4 km).

You continue on the Baldwin Point Trail through a stand of white birch to a vista at 2.2 miles (3.5 km). Here you look west and north over the Baldwin and County Line branches of Young Womans Creek, which flow into the West Branch of the Susquehanna at North Bend. Several specimens of red pine grow to one side of the overlook. These appear to be wild (that is, not planted) and at this point are fairly close to the southern limit of their range. Red pine seen much to the south of here usually have been planted.

To continue the hike return to the junction with the Refuge Trail and turn left, or east, to follow it downhill into Yellow Jacket Hollow where it joins the Black Forest Trail. The Black Forest Trail is blazed with orange dots, and you follow them up the other side of the hollow past a trail register.

At 4.7 miles (7.6 km) you cross PA 44 and continue on Trout Run Road for .3 mile (500 meters) to a vista of Naval Run, Hemlock Mountain, and Gas Line Ridge. These areas are also visited or viewed on the Black Forest Trail (Hike 43). You now take the trail into the woods and soon cross and follow the headwaters of Trout Run. At 5.7 miles (9.2 km) you pass an old beaver dam and shortly thereafter reach Boyer Mill Road. Here you leave the trail by turning right on this low-use, unpaved road. The sign here is in error by a factor of almost 2. It is only .8 mile (1.3 km) to PA 44, not 1.5 miles.

As soon as you approach PA 44 cut across the intervening ground, cross the highway, and pick up the blue-blazed Baldwin Point Trail at the vehicle gate. You dip down into the headwaters of Yellow Jacket Hollow, passing close by two springs. You regain the plateau after a short climb and continue to a trail junction at 7.5 miles (12.1 km). Turn left on the unblazed trail for the walk back to your car.

40 Splash Dam Hollow

Total distance: 8.6 miles (13.8 km)
Walking time: 5 hours
Vertical rise: 960 feet (290 meters)

Along the trail

The Susquehannock Trail System opened for hiking in 1969. Most of this giant loop trail lies within Potter County, but it does stray over the line into Clinton County in three or four places. The system passes through Patterson Picnic Area and Ole Bull State Park, and skirts Prouty Picnic Area, Lyman Run State Park, and Cherry Springs State Park. It also traverses the Hammersley Wild Area. Part of this circuit hike includes an unblazed, little-used trail for which you may need your compass.

The trailhead is the system's Northern Gateway on US 6, located 2.6 miles west of Denton Hill Ski Area and Pennsylvania Lumber Museum. Allow time to visit the museum and its exhibits. They will enhance your knowledge of the logging industry in this and other areas of Penn's Woods. Seeing the old Shay logging locomotive itself is worth the small admission price. At the trailhead drive down the side road and park well off the highway. Plenty of space lies at the field's edge beyond the fringe of woods.

Begin by following the orange-blazed Ridge Trail for .6 mile (950 meters) and then turn right on White Line Trail, also orange blazed. You find the flat trail, which follows a former border of state forest land, really allows you to swing along. The cloverlike plant on the ground is oxalis, or wood sorrel, and the oxalic acid in its juice accounts for its sharp taste. Pioneers short of salt are said to have substituted extract of oxalis. They must have been either desperate or unaware that

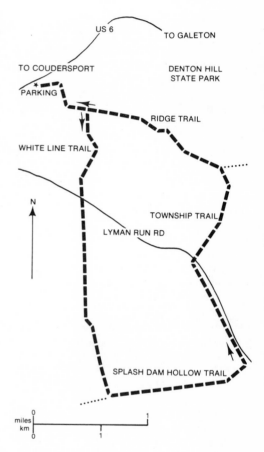

oxalic acid is poisonous.

At 1.4 miles (2.3 km) you cross Lyman Run Road, then a jeep road, and next begin the long descent into Splash Dam Hollow. At the junction with the Splash Dam Trail the Susquehannock turns right and you turn left. The new trail, an easily followed old road, becomes even more distinct as you move downstream. Evidence of considerable beaver activity exists along the stream and the animals may be partly responsible for the open meadows along the hollow. There is no sign of a splash dam but trout fishermen report old timbers in a deep pool near the junction with Lyman Run. At 4 miles (6.5 km) another old grade comes in from your left and is soon followed by another. Along these lower stretches you see evidence of four-wheel vehicles. Finally, at 4.5 miles (7.3 km), you cross Lyman Run at a ford and follow Lyman Run Road to the left for 1.1 miles (1.8 km) of road walking.

At 5.7 miles (9.1 km) turn right on the signed, unblazed, and little-used Township Trail. As the footway becomes obscure, continue up the bottom of the hollow to the flat ridge top, bear slightly left, and continue almost due north. With sharp eyes you may find a faint trace of footway marked with axe blazes so old the bark has completely healed across them. However, the woods are open and you don't really need the trail. Toward the far side of the wide ridge you run into the heavily used and orange-blazed Susquehannock Trail. If you unknowingly cross the trail you quickly descend into Elm Hollow to a bulldozed vehicle trail you can't miss. In either case, turn left as the two routes join at 7 miles (11.4 km).

At 8 miles (12.8 km) you reach the Susquehannock Trail System junction and retrace the hike's first stretch back to your car.

41 Kettle Creek Vista

Total distance: 8.7 miles (13.9 km)
Walking time: 5 hours
Vertical rise: 1,420 feet (430 meters)

The red-blazed Donut Hole Trail, a part of this hike, winds across Sproul State Forest, linking the Susquehannock and Quehanna trails as well as Hyner Run and Kettle Creek state parks. The name Donut Hole is a joke among employees of the Bureau of Forestry, who regard Sproul District as the doughnut hole of the bureau. Certainly the human inhabitants of the district are outnumbered by the deer, and perhaps even the bears. But those who like to hunt, fish, or hike find Sproul State Forest loaded with attractions.

The hike's trailhead is the same as that for Summerson Run and Owl Hollow (see Hike 35). Follow PA 120 to Westport and turn north onto the road immediately to the east of the one-lane bridge over Kettle Creek. This is Kettle Creek Road, which you follow for 6 miles.

Park just beyond the main entrance to Kettle Creek State Park in the lot on the east side of the road. Trail Blazes for the Donut Hole cross some of the sites in the campground so make your way downstream on the park road and pick up the blazes again where the trail crosses Kettle Creek on a substantial footbridge of steel I-beams.

At the far side turn right along the water's edge, cross the dam abutment, and about 60 yards (60 meters) farther take a sharp left on the Hicks Hollow Trail and start climbing. You soon leave the Hicks Hollow Trail and turn sharply right on a new trail cut for the

Donut Hole. Continue climbing and pass through an extensive hemlock stand similar to those of Pennsylvania's Black Forest of a century ago. The crew that built this trail section surely did its rock work! This section, as well as another farther along, is an example of how to do trail construction on Pennsylvania's rocky hillsides without the aid of mechanized equipment. All trail building and maintenance groups should hike these sections. The rough but stable footway is reasonably easy to walk but still uneven enough to discourage use by motorcycles and other off-road motorized devices.

At 1.4 miles (2.2 km) you drop down a bit, turn left uphill on the Honey Run Trail, and see its pretty little stream running down the isolated valley. At 1.6 miles (2.6 km) the old trail splits; you follow the right branch, which has been reconstructed along the hillside. As you climb notice the large, tabular sandstone boulders above the trail. Finally, this new trail joins an old woods road and the climbing eases off a bit. At 3.2 miles (5.1 km) you reach a trail register; the Crowley Road is just beyond.

Turn right and follow the little-used Crowley Road for .2 mile (400 meters) to a junction with the road to Kettle Creek Vista, another .4 mile (700 meters) ahead. Just before you reach the vista notice a natural gas well on your right. It is part of the long-exhausted Leidy Field, now used for gas storage.

Kettle Creek Vista from Donut Hole Trail

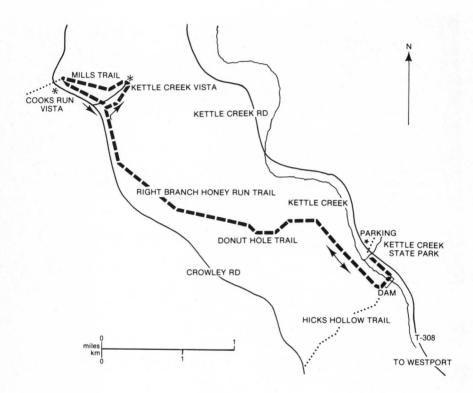

From the vista you see over the waters impounded by Bush Dam and far up Kettle Creek Valley. The dam, to your right, is one of several earthfill flood-control dams in the West Branch river basin. During a flood the water level could rise well above the recreational level before overflowing.

Continue following the red-blazed Mills Trail into the woods. At 4.8 miles (7.7 km) you leave the Donut Hole Trail and turn left on the Crowley Road, where you reach a vista over Cooks Run to the southwest. At 5.2 miles (8.3 km) you again reach the Kettle Creek Vista road on your left. Continue ahead on the Donut Hole Trail along Crowley Road and retrace your steps to your car.

Indian pipes

42 Golden Eagle Trail

Total distance: 8.9 miles (14.4 km)
Walking time: 6½ hours
Vertical rise: 2,100 feet (640 meters)

The Golden Eagle Trail may be the best day hike in Penn's Woods. It has everything: mountain streams, big trees, mountain laurel, relics from the logging days, views of wild and pastoral landscapes, meadows, small waterfalls, and, of course, Pine Creek. Overnight camping is not permitted on the rugged trail since the few available sites would suffer from overuse.

The trail is on State Game Land 68 and in Tiadaghton State Forest, where it traverses the Wolf Run Wild Area. To reach the trail drive north on PA 414 for 2.7 miles beyond the village of Cammal and park on the roadside. You begin the trail, marked with circular orange blazes, by crossing the railroad tracks, then climbing the ledge, and heading upstream along Wolf Run. Turn left almost immediately and cross the run on a footbridge. Be grateful for

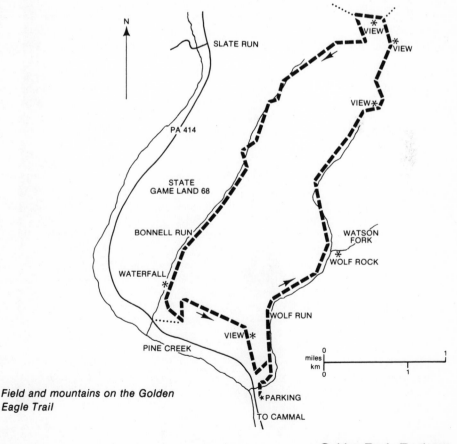

Field and mountains on the Golden Eagle Trail

this bridge—it is the only one you're going to see on Wolf Run. You next pass an old quarry and the junction with the return portion of the trail. Continue up the run. Crossings are now fairly frequent, and you see several small waterfalls along here.

At .8 mile (1.3 km) in the hollow on the left you see remains of an old log skid. Logs were often slid down the sides of steep hills to a railroad or a stream for transportation to Williamsport. At. 1.4 miles (2.3 km) Watson Fork comes in from the east with Wolf Rock, a natural overlook to its south. No trail runs to Wolf Rock but if you move up Watson Fork a short distance and then scramble up the steep slope to your right, you can reach the top. If the trees have dropped their leaves, you will have a good view of Wolf Run Valley.

At 2.1 miles (3.4 km) you reach an old logging camp marked by large white pines and hemlocks and the remains of the old camp stove. Evidently the loggers were reluctant to cut trees in the immediate vicinity of their camp. Wolf Run becomes intermittent above this point. You soon move out of the hollow and reach the first vista at 2.9 miles (4.7 km) to look west over the top of Wolf Run and across Bonnell Run to Black Forest Trail country on the far side of Pine Creek.

You then continue up the ridge line and cross into State Game Land 68 for a view east over the fields of Beulahland. At about 2,160 feet (665 meters), this is the highest point on the trail. At 3.7 miles (6 km), turn left for a second view west across Bonnell Run and Black Forest Trail country. The Golden Eagle then slants down into the saddle, where it turns left into Bonnell Run. At 4.3 miles (6.9 km) a spring lies about 15 yards (15 meters) left of the trail, but you find another and better one at 4.7 miles (7.6 km). Continue down Bonnell Run and cross back into state forest land at 5.9 miles (9.5 km). Soon the run enters a small gorge and you veer slowly away from it. At 6.9 miles (11.1 km) you bear left on a newly cut trail. At this point a small waterfall lies at the bottom of a steep descent to Bonnell Run. You now climb gently to the edge of Clark's Pasture for a view down Pine Creek, then follow the field's edge to an old quarry road, and begin a serious climb to the ridge between Wolf Run and Pine Creek at 7.9 miles (12.7 km).

The first vista to the left of the trail has a good view up Wolf Run. The second vista is from a rock called the Raven's Horn, which is a roosting spot for ravens and has views of both Wolf Run and Pine Creek. The third and last vista has views up and down Pine Creek. You then descend on steep switchbacks before turning left off the ridge into Wolf Run. Continue descending to the trail coming up Wolf Run at 8.6 miles (13.9 km). Turn right for the brief journey back to PA 414.

43 Black Forest Trail

Total distance: 9.8 miles (15.8 km)
Walking time: 5½ hours
Vertical rise: 1,220 feet (370 meters)

Fast water in early spring

This hike treats you to a section of the famous Black Forest Trail along Pine Creek Gorge. Your route goes past a waterfall, views, and the historic remains of the Cammal and Black Forest Railroad, built to log much of this area.

The hike's trailhead was once a pumping station of the Tidewater Petroleum pipeline, the first successful long-distance pipeline in the world. The pumps here were powered by a steam engine; coal to fire it was transported on the Cammal and Black Forest. When the railroad ceased operating a natural gas well was drilled at Slate Run and a short pipeline was run from there to the pump station to keep the steam engine going. The Tidewater pipeline, tiny by today's standards, is no longer in use, but you can see remains of it in several road cuts along PA 44, particularly to the north of the pump station. The pipeline was built in 1879 but the pump station was presumably built later as the Cammal and Black Forest didn't reach it until 1894 or 1895.

To reach the trailhead drive north on PA 44 for 12.9 miles from the junction with PA 664 in Haneyville. Turn right on the Manor Fork Road, drive past a couple of hunting camps, and park at the Winter Sports parking area at the far side of the clearing.

Start walking on Manor Fork Road and then bear right with blue blazes at the vehicle gate. This is the Gas Line Trail, which follows the route of the old gas pipeline from State Run.

At 1.2 miles (2 km) you continue ahead on the orange-blazed Black Forest Trail, which comes in from your left. After 200 yards (200 meters) turn left for White Birch Lookout. This vista is a bit off the main trail but don't pass it by unless the ridge is really socked in by dense fog. White Birch looks north over Little Slate Run Valley. Moss Hollow Lookout, another 200 yards (200 meters) or so along the trail, looks south over Naval Run to Hemlock Mountain. At 2 miles (3.3 km) you bear right for Canyon Vista, .4 mile farther on. In front of you the ground falls away into Naval Run, revealing Pine Creek, the famous gorge far to the south, and the hills beyond. This is one of the three or four best views on the Black Forest Trail.

When you can tear yourself away from Canyon Vista, continue past Naval Run View to the west and Lookout Ledge, where you see Pine Creek Gorge to the north and the tiny village of Slate Run. Next is a view of Hemlock Mountain to the southwest. You then bear right and switch back down into Naval Run.

At the bottom head upstream above Naval Run. The waterfall, at 4.5 miles (7.2 km), is visible from the trail but you have to descend the steep bank to the edge of the overhang to get a really good look. This part of the state was never glaciated and waterfalls are rare.

At 5.1 miles (8.2 km) you leave the trail where it crosses the run on a log bridge. Don't cross but continue upstream as best you can some 50 yards (50 meters) and then bear right

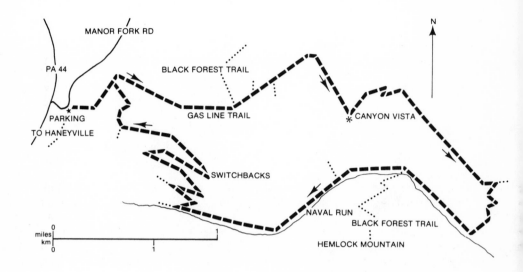

on the wide but unblazed fire road that crosses the run at this point. Heading upstream, you follow this delightful little stream as it tinkles over the moss-covered rocks and sparkles in the sun.

Your next turn onto railroad switchbacks is not marked and requires special attention. As you walk up the fire road along the run you cross a side stream from Moss Hollow. The fire road is then quite straight for over .6 mile (1 km). When it finally bends to the right, start looking uphill on your right to find the old railroad grade coming down. It reaches the bottom at a dry run from the right. (The fire road continues upstream past this point.)

Take a sharp right onto the railroad grade at this first switchback and start your easy but protracted climb out of Naval Run. Judging from the length of the spur at the second switchback,

only two log cars at a time could have been brought up this grade. The third switchback has been complicated by quarrying operations. A quarry road continues ahead but is steeper and less smooth than the old railroad grade. Turn sharply right again and follow the grade through one quarry and then above another one. From here on it is smooth sailing past the fourth, fifth, and sixth switchbacks.

At 9.2 miles (14.8 km) you reach a log gate across the old grade. Turn right just beyond the gate and pass in front of the Naval Run Hunting Camp 12-C-79. This starts you out on an old road that quickly becomes overgrown with mountain laurel. The trail first swings off to the right and then turns sharply to the left for the short distance back to the blue-blazed Gas Line Trail. Turn left on the Gas Line Trail, and in .3 mile (500 meters) you are at your car.

44 Asaph Wild Area

Total distance: 9.9 miles (15.9 km)
Walking time: 6 hours
Vertical rise: 1,270 feet (390 meters)

Skunk cabbage

In the northern reaches of Tioga State Forest lie a small wild area and contiguous natural area that provide the setting for a challenging day hike—but not if it's your first time out. You need skill in following unblazed trails and making one short bushwhack. Some of the trail junctions are marked only with signs, so you may feel better with your compass in your pack.

The circuit hike begins and ends at the Asaph Run State Forest Picnic Area at the forks of Asaph Run. The area is reached from US 6 between PA 287 and PA 362. Turn north over Marsh Creek at the sign for Asaph

Village, .2 miles farther turn left at a stop sign, and after another .5 mile bear right just before the road recrosses the railroad tracks and drive 2.7 miles to the picnic area. Plenty of parking space and camping area lie on the far side of Asaph Run.

Start across Right Asaph Run and head up the middle ridge trail. Left Asaph Run drops below and occasionally you glimpse the canyon's far side. At .9 mile (1.5 km) take the trail's left fork and farther along keep right at the edge of a clearing with old apple trees. The trees suggest this was once a logging camp. The grade up the side

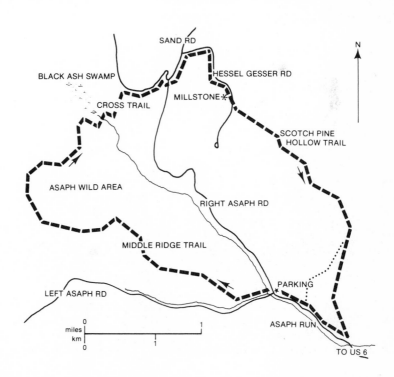

of middle ridge is too variable for a logging railroad, but as you reach an obscure trail junction at 3 miles (4.9 km) you see you are on an old railroad grade.

The grade winds around the head of Roberts Branch before it heads straight into Black Ash Swamp—and disappears. The swamp is an old beaver meadow surrounded by hardwoods. You now start to bushwhack for .3 mile (500 meters). Turn right around the swamp edge and follow it to the outlet. Cross the outlet, which is usually quite small, and head downstream across a boggy meadow to trees at the far side, where you find old trail signs. Turn left on the Cross Trail and follow it uphill to 4.6 miles (7.4 km), where you turn right on a nameless road for .6 mile (900 meters) to a junction with Sand Road and Right Asaph Road. To shorten your hike turn right down Right Asaph Road; to continue turn left up Sand Road and .3 mile (500 meters) farther turn right on Hessel Gesser Road.

After .6 mile (1 km) watch on your right for an outcrop of coarse sandstone and conglomerate. This is the site of the Hessel Gesser millstone, which is marked with a large signboard. In the 1830s James Hessel Gesser cut stones here for gristmills in Tioga and Potter counties. This blank evidently had no buyer. Gristmills were not runaway successes, and according to county records, those in Tioga County soon closed "for lack of a profitable clientele."

The Hessel Gesser Road is gated to vehicles just beyond the millstone, but you continue and just before the road swings right bear left on the unmarked Scotch Pine Hollow Trail. At first this trail shows use by four-wheel vehicles, but as you swing along the broad ridge top the trail narrows. You encounter a small run flowing left across the trail towards Straight Run, and continue past Darling Road Trail on the left at 7.8 miles (12.5 km) to descend into Scotch Pine Hollow. You cross the run shortly, bear right at a conspicuous fork at 8.6 miles (13.8 km), and at 9 miles (14.5 km) you hit Asaph Road.

Turn right on the road and walk .9 mile (1.4 km) back to your car. Along the way you pass another, steeper version of the Scotch Pine Hollow Trail that follows the run down to the road.

45 Hammersley Wild Area

Total distance: 10.5 miles (16.9 km)
Walking time: 6 hours
Vertical rise: 900 feet (275 meters)

Deep pool on the Hammersley

Your trek here is through one of the two largest roadless areas in the state. Although the 31,000 acres of the Hammersley are managed by the Bureau of Forestry as a wild area, it cannot be officially designated as one because the state does not own the mineral rights. The Susquehannock Trail traverses the Hammersley, and this section is its longest (10 miles/16 km) that does not cross a road.

The Hammersley was not always so wild. At the turn of the century it was laced with railroads and even supported a town where the Nelson Branch joins the Hammersley Fork. Most of the trails through the wild area are old railroad grades.

The Hammersley is widely known for its rattlesnakes. About half of all the rattlesnakes I've encountered in Penn's Woods have been here, so do watch your step.

You need a car shuttle. Leave one car in the lot in the village of Cross Fork on PA 144, just north of the Clinton-Potter county line. (At the turn of the century, this tiny town had scheduled rail service, stave and lumber mills, and a population of thousands.) To reach the other end of this hike from Cross Fork follow PA 144 left for over .5 mile, and then bear right on Cross Fork Creek Road for 3.9 miles. Turn left on Windfall Road and drive for 3.8 miles to Red Ridge Road, and turn left. After another 3.6 miles turn left yet again onto McConnell Road. About 2 miles down the road you pass a vista of the upper Hammersley area and Elk Lick Knob. The

Susquehannock Trail crossing is just .3 mile farther, and you can park along the road.

Start your hike down the orange-blazed Hammersley Trail, as the Susquehannock is here called. After .8 mile (1.3 km), you reach the first of a series of meadows. At least one active beaver colony can usually be found here along the upper part of the Hammersley. Also note the apple trees, which legends say grew from apple cores thrown away by lumberjacks.

A pipeline swath is at 1.4 miles (2.3 km). Wild area designation would protect the Hammersley from crossings by any more such rights-of-way. Soon you pass Black Mark Hollow, named for a black mark made by Indians on a tree at the hollow's mouth.

Stonework bridge abutments are still visible at several places where the old railroad grade crosses side streams. You cross Bunnell Run at 3.3 miles (5.3 km) and shortly the Bunnell Ridge Trail, and then Road Hollow Run and its trail at 4.2 miles (6.7 km). Road Hollow is named for the railroad that ran here.

Shortly you cross the Hammersley Fork itself. Most of the season you can hop on rocks but in higher water you might have to wade across. Scramble up the steep bank on the far side. The trail stays well up the side of the valley from here to Dry Hollow, at 5 miles (8.1 km). Despite its name a good flow of water usually exits from Dry Hollow, and at one time there was a splash

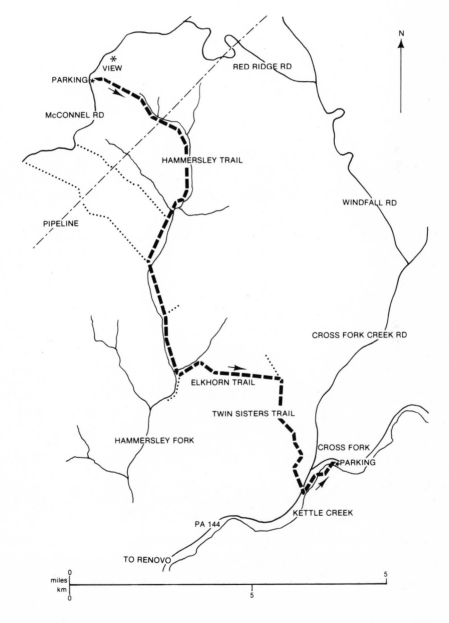

N

VIEW

PARKING

RED RIDGE RD

McCONNEL RD

HAMMERSLEY TRAIL

WINDFALL RD

PIPELINE

CROSS FORK CREEK RD

ELKHORN TRAIL

TWIN SISTERS TRAIL

HAMMERSLEY FORK

CROSS FORK

PARKING

KETTLE CREEK

PA 144

TO RENOVO

miles
km

0
0
5
5

Hammersley Wild Area 163

dam here.

Just beyond, you reach a cascade and pool, one of the gems of the Hammersley. The water here is deep enough for swimming even in mid-summer. Downstream from this pool you climb again, pass a trail register, and finally return to water level at the mouth of Elkhorn Hollow.

Here you follow the blazes left uphill on the Elkhorn Trail and start the big climb of the day. At first you follow the run, but at 6.4 miles (10.3 km) you bear right up a steep bank and start the real climb. Towards the top the grade eases off, but you continue climbing until 7.6 miles (12.2 km).

Shortly after reaching the crest you turn right onto the Twin Sisters Trail, named for Twin Sisters Hollow, which in turn was named for two giant pines that once grew there. Now you can really swing along through the luxuriant thickets of mountain laurel to reach one of the handful of vistas on the Susquehannock Trail at 8.9 miles (14.2 km). You have an extensive view over the village of Cross Fork and up Kettle Creek and Cross Fork.

From here it's all downhill along the old Lackawanna Lumber Company railroad grade to PA 144, where you follow the blazes left along the highway a short distance to a gravel road. Bear right to Keener Camp and then right again at the end of the road to the Ten Pines footbridge across Kettle Creek. From the far end of the bridge it is only .2 mile (300 meters) through the meadows back to the parking lot at the edge of Cross Fork.

Backpacking
Trips

46 Chuck Keiper Trail/East Loop

Time allowed: 2 days, 1 night
Total distance: 16.6 miles (26.8 km)
Walking time: 11 hours
Vertical rise: 2,850 feet (870 meters)

In the late 1960s the part of Sproul State Forest you hike through on this trip was threatened by Project Ketch of the Atomic Energy Commission's Plowshare Program. Project Ketch called for the underground explosion of more than one thousand hydrogen bombs to create underground chambers for natural gas storage. Fortunately, citizen protest groups stopped Ketch before the first bomb was detonated.

Along the trail you encounter native cranberries, old growth hemlock, and two small mountain bogs set aside as natural areas. Like other parts of the Chuck Keiper Trail, this section should be hiked when water levels are low. Free maps of the trail can be obtained from the Sproul State Forest, Star Route, Shintown, Renovo, PA 17764.

This two-day trek begins at the East Branch Trail on PA 144 21 miles northeast of PA 879 and 9.6 miles south of PA 120 in Renovo. There's no parking at the trailhead but there is space off PA 144 opposite Swamp Branch Road .6 mile to the southwest. A short car shuttle is necessary to spot a second car at Diamond Rock Trail, 4.1 miles north on PA 144. Park here at a wide spot on the road's east side, immediately north of the trail junction.

First Day

East Branch Trail to Sled Road Hollow
Distance: 8.9 miles (14.2 km)
Walking time: 6 hours

Backpackers on the Chuck Keiper Trail

Begin your adventure by following the yellow blazes of the East Branch Trail through an evergreen plantation. After about 200 yards (200 meters) you cross a pipeline swath and continue along the border of East Branch Swamp Natural Area. Shortly after passing a trail register, jog right on Coon Run Road and then continue on the far side of the East Branch of Big Run. In recent years a beaver colony has been active along this stretch of the stream.

At 1.6 miles (2.5 km) you join an old logging railroad grade and follow it across three log bridges over the East Branch to a major trail junction marked by a triple blaze at 2.4 miles (3.8 km). The west loop of the Chuck Keiper Trail goes right here, but you turn left on the east loop. Continue along the white-blazed edge of state forest land and past a large salvage cut on the left. Then jog left at Beech Creek Road and cross another large salvage cut. At the far edge your route swings left onto the Four Ridge Trail, enters the woods, and at 3.6 miles (5.8 km) crosses a bridge over Rock Run. After a short climb, again along the state forest boundary, bear left on another old trail. At 4.4 miles (7.1 km) cross Shoemaker Ridge Road and a small stream, and then climb over a hill to the Clendenin Branch at 5.2 miles (8.4 km).

After negotiating the Clendenin Branch on a log bridge you begin your first real climb. Cranberry Run, which you reach at 6.6 miles (10.7 km) makes a reasonable backup campsite if you

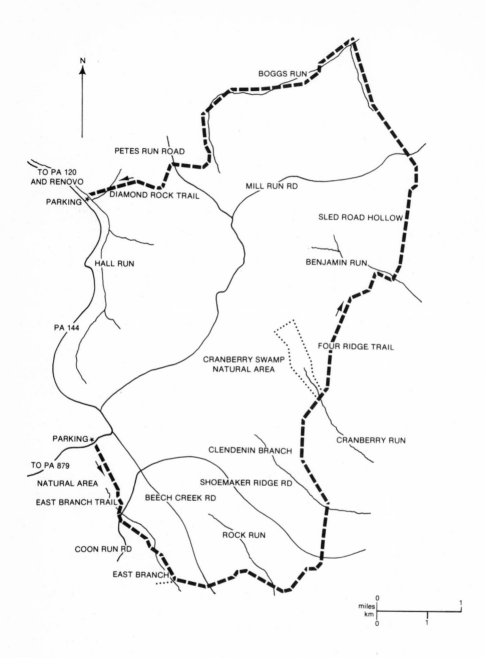

N

BOGGS RUN

PETES RUN ROAD

TO PA 120
AND RENOVO

PARKING

DIAMOND ROCK TRAIL

MILL RUN RD

SLED ROAD HOLLOW

HALL RUN

BENJAMIN RUN

PA 144

FOUR RIDGE TRAIL

CRANBERRY SWAMP
NATURAL AREA

CRANBERRY RUN

PARKING

CLENDENIN BRANCH

TO PA 879

NATURAL AREA

SHOEMAKER RIDGE RD

EAST BRANCH TRAIL

BEECH CREEK RD

ROCK RUN

COON RUN RD

EAST BRANCH

0
miles
km
0
1
1

are pressed by darkness. If you camp here, walk the white-blazed loop trail 2.4 miles (3.8 km) around Cranberry Swamp Natural Area as dusk approaches when deer will be out in force. If you just want a quick peek at Cranberry Swamp, then cross the run, drop your pack, and follow the white-blazed trail a short distance to a spot where you look out across the bog.

There's a second good climb beyond Cranberry Run. Part way down the far side you've a view over Benjamin Run and up Sled Road Hollow. Continuing, you pick up a woods road and follow a jeep road to the edge of Benjamin Run, where you turn downstream for some 300 yards (300 meters) before finally crossing. After passing a hunting camp with a piped spring you head up Sled Road Hollow. You are not permitted to stay at the leased hunting camp without permission of the owners, so look for a good spot to camp once you are beyond sight of it.

Second Day

Sled Road Hollow to Diamond Rock Trail
Distance: 7.7 miles (12.6 km)
Walking time: 5 hours

This morning you continue the climb up Sled Road Hollow. Once you leave the stream behind, the trail becomes steeper and then joins a jeep road, which you follow uphill to Mill Run Road at 10.2 miles (16.4 km). A view over Boggs Run is up Mill Run Road to the left. Boggs Run is the wildest and least-traveled portion of the Chuck Keiper Trail, but for obscure reasons is not officially designated a wild area.

Cross the road and start the long grade down to Boggs Run. Notice the many white birch along this section. A possible campsite is at 11.1 miles (17.8 km) where the trail crosses and then immediately recrosses the stream. At 11.7 miles (19.1 km) you reach Boggs Run itself and turn left upstream for the long climb out of the canyon. Here you find continuous campsites for several miles upstream. Along much of Boggs Run you follow the grade of an old logging railroad, and in places you can still see the old ties.

A very tricky spot lies at 14 miles (22.5 km). The trail suddenly turns right and moves straight up the side of the canyon, but after only 135 yards (125 meters) it turns left on another grade. This one is level and Boggs Run comes up to meet it farther upstream.

At 14.7 miles (23.7 km) the trail finally turns up a side hollow and regains the plateau. You jog left on Petes Run Road at 15.3 miles (24.6 km) and then turn right on the Diamond Rock Trail to enter a clearcut with a view of Diamond Rock Hollow and Hall Run. Look closely for the turn where the trail bears right off the jeep road and descends sharply. No camping is permitted in Diamond Rock Hollow as it is part of the drainage system for Renovo's water supply. Finally you cross a side stream on rocks and then Hall Run itself on a log bridge to arrive at the edge of PA 144 and the end of this adventure in Penn's Woods.

47 Lost Turkey Trail

Time allowed: 2 days, 1 night
Total distance: 17.4 miles (28.1 km)
Walking time: 11 hours
Vertical rise: 2,400 feet (730 meters)

The Lost Turkey Trail east of Johnstown moves through hardwood forests and follows many old logging railroad grades. Because of the elevation of this part of the Allegheny Plateau, hemlock and hardwoods such as beech and black cherry grow here, well to the south of other such forests. Despite the forest's proximity to the main line of the Pennsylvania Railroad, the trees were not immediately exploited. The optimal railroad route led up the South Fork of the Conemaugh River, which was blocked by a dam built to supply water to the Pennsylvania Canal. The dam outlived the canal and the area became a rustic retreat for the very rich. It was this dam that burst on May 31, 1889, producing the first Johnstown Flood. Within a year a railroad had been laid through the gap and the cutting of the virgin forests along the Cambria-Somerset border was underway.

In 1976 Youth Conservation Corps crews blazed the Lost Turkey Trail from Blue Knob Fire Tower to Babcock Picnic Area on PA 56. The trail was named by the crews and the story behind the name shall remain untold to save embarrassment to the two experienced woods persons who scouted the route. The trail crosses state park, game and forest land, as well as private land. For a free map of Lost Turkey Trail (and adjoining John P. Saylor Trail, Hike 15), write to Blue Knob State Park, RD 1, Imler, PA 16655.

Beaver lodge

Spot one car at the Babcock Picnic Area on PA 56 east of Windber. Notify the Windber Police Department you are leaving it there. In a second car drive east on PA 56 for 11.1 miles, bear left on PA 96 in Pleasantville for 4.3 miles, and then turn left on PA 869 in Weyant. You reach Pavia in 3.5 miles and should turn off there for the Blue Knob park office to tell attendants you are leaving a car at Burnt House Picnic Area. Then return to Pavia, turn right on PA 869, and drive 2.2 miles to that picnic area.

First Day

Burnt House Picnic Area to Clear Shade Creek
Distance: 10.1 miles (16.3 km)
Walking time: 7 hours

The red-blazed Lost Turkey Trail has little water so fill your canteen from the piped spring at the base of the slope near the picnic area shelter. The metric distances given here match the trail's kilometer posts; mileages given refer to the distance you actually have walked.

Pick up the trail at the PA 869 bridge for Wallacks Branch. You are 14.2 kilometers from Lost Turkey's start at the Blue Knob Fire Tower. Soon bear left onto an old railroad grade built by the South Fork Lumber Company of Allendale, and follow it for most of the climb up the Allegheny Front, which starts here in Big Break Hollow. Keep left where the trail splits. (A relocation appears to have been made at this point.) Soon you pass the 15-kilometer post (.5 mile) and enter State Game Land 26. You cross Big Break Run on a pair of elaborate footbridges and pass back and forth between game and park land many times before reaching the top of the hill.

At 15.6 kilometers (.9 mile) there's a view of Big Break Hollow. You then take a sharp left at a switchback, come upon another view down the hollow, and switch back to the right. After Post 18 the trail levels off a bit, but at 19.3 kilometers (3.2 miles) it switches sharply left and turns upward again. At 20.3 kilometers (3.8 miles) you pass through a poison ivy patch and finally reach the hilltop.

At 21 kilometers (4.2 miles) you reach the edge of a small meadow in State Game Land 26. Bear right and take the obvious exit from the meadow; then turn left on a snowmobile trail that soon crosses onto private land and picks up another old railroad grade of the South Fork Lumber Company. Next you cross a good stream that flows right, into a beaver pond. Fairly continuous meadows along this stretch are well dotted with low-bush blueberry.

At 23.8 kilometers (6 miles), in the middle of a large meadow, turn left off the old railroad grade, cross a stream, and head upstream a short distance to a jeep road. Start a gentle climb out of this valley, and then follow a succession of jeep roads, some of which go along the very edge of the Allegheny Front.

At 26.5 kilometers (7.4 miles) you cross a jeep road with a view to the

left over the Front and then head into the woods along little or no footway. The trail winds and twists through dense woods at the edge of the front, so watch closely for blazes. At 27.5 kilometers (8.3 miles) you pick up the white-blazed boundary of the Gallitzen State Forest and follow it to 27.9 kilometers (8.5 miles), where you turn left on a jeep road to a junction with T-779 and Buffalo Road. Continue straight ahead on Buffalo Road to 28.6 kilometers (8.9 miles), where you keep right, cross a small stream, and turn left on a woods road.

You reach a small clearing at 29.4 kilometers (9.4 miles), but do not camp here as Buffalo Road is just to your left. Turn right and climb over a low ridge to a stream crossing and the first and just about the only feasible campsite on the whole trail. Pitch your tent away from the trail. Buffalo Road is close but there is no direct access from it. In the wet seasons you might want to camp farther upstream.

Second Day

Clear Shade Creek to Babcock Picnic Area
Distance: 7.3 miles (11.8 km)
Walking time: 4 hours

As you swing along the trail up the hollow you soon notice you are on an old railroad grade, one in the far-ranging railroad network built by the Babcock Lumber Company. E. V. Babcock once put this system to unique use. During his courting of Mary Dundore Arnold of Reading, he converted

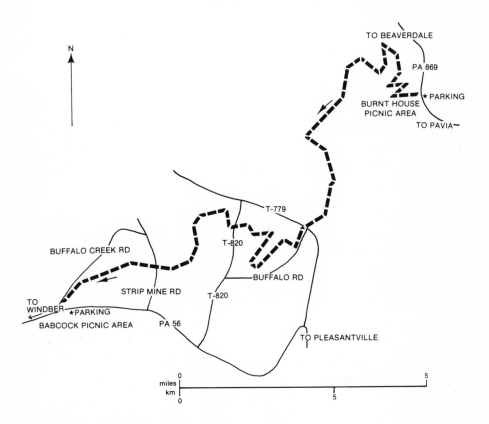

several log cars to flat cars, imported a
Meyer Davis orchestra from Philadelphia, and took his intended on
a moonlight tour of his forest. How the
orchestra ever played over the puffing
of a Shay locomotive, I do not know.
After all that, what could Mary say but
"Yes"!

At the end of the hollow you head
left along the white-blazed state forest
boundary and then cross another hollow. You cross the dirt road, T-820, at
32.9 kilometers (11.6 miles) and the
main branch of Clear Shade Creek
immediately beyond. Swing right,
climb to the broad top of Pot Ridge,

and just beyond the 35-kilometer post
(12.9 miles) turn left on another railroad grade in the middle of a meadow.
Cross Strip Mine Road at 37.7 kilometers (14.6 miles) and continue
through the woods on obscure footway. At 38.4 kilometers (15 miles) bear
left on a bull-dozed road and then
shortly left onto a grassy road. From
here you follow old roads and jeep
roads to 39.7 kilometers (15.8 miles),
where you turn left on Babcock Creek
Road. Follow it to PA 56 across from
the Babcock Picnic Area and your car.

Lost Turkey Trail 173

48 Hyner Run to Ole Bull

Time allowed: 2 days, 1 night
Total distance: 22.6 miles (36.3 km)
Walking time: 14 hours
Vertical rise: 4,500 feet (1,370 meters)

This hike includes parts of the Donut Hole and Susquehannock trails in its route between Hyner Run and Ole Bull state parks. The latter is named for Ole Borneman Bull, a world-famous Norwegian violinist who in 1852 purchased 11,000 acres here in Potter County from an American swindler and proceeded to establish a settlement for Norwegian colonists. At that time Norway was one of the poorest countries in the world, and some eight hundred colonists moved here before the actual owner discovered the land ruse. He offered to sell his land to Bull at a very low price but by then the tide had turned on the Norwegian's fortunes. Most of the colonists moved on to Wisconsin, but some stayed in Potter County and their descendants live here today.

Free maps of the Donut Hole Trail and the relevant part of the Susquehannock Trail are available from the Sproul State Forest, Star Route, Shintown, Renovo, PA 17764.

This hike requires a car shuttle, with one car at Ole Bull State Park on PA 144 a few miles south of the PA 44 junction at Oleona. Check in with attendants at the park office for parking instructions. Then drive your second car south on PA 144 and turn left on PA 120 just west of Renovo. Continue east through Renovo and turn north to Hyner Run State Park in the village of Hyner, for a total driving distance of 35.6 miles. Check in at the

Deer crossing the road

office at this end also for parking directions.

First Day

Hyner Run State Park to Bull Run
Distance: 11.4 miles (18.3 km)
Walking Time: 7 hours
    You start on the Donut Hole Trail at a sign just beyond the park swimming pool, following red blazes up Log Hollow Trail. You soon pass a trail register and power-line swath, and then climb steadily and easily along the old road grade to the plateau. At 1.7 miles (2.7 km) turn right onto Fye Camp Trail and cross the Long Fork and its trail at 2.5 miles (4 km). Just beyond, you enter a large salvage cut; watch blazes carefully on this stretch. Shad bushes and an occasional pitch pine are the only things along here the oak-leaf roller has left alive.

Beyond the clearcut you drop sharply to a tributary of Abes Run and drop again to cross the run and Abes Fork Road at 3.7 miles (6 km). You then follow switchbacks up the far side to regain the plateau. At the next stream descend on switchbacks and cross Cougar Run at 5.2 miles (8.4 km). This name is a corruption of Koughler, a German immigrant and Civil War veteran who ran a trap line up this run in the last century.

Turn left up the run and pass a possible campsite at 5.5 miles (8.8 km), where a side stream comes in from the right. Toward the top of Cougar Run turn left near a hunting camp and follow its access road across Dry Run Road at 6.2 miles (10 km). Continue

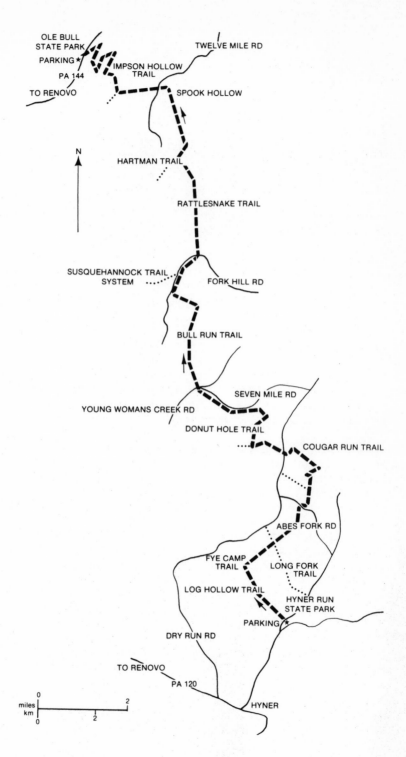

OLE BULL
STATE PARK

PARKING ★

PA 144

TO RENOVO

TWELVE MILE RD

IMPSON HOLLOW
TRAIL

SPOOK HOLLOW

N

HARTMAN TRAIL

RATTLESNAKE TRAIL

SUSQUEHANNOCK TRAIL
SYSTEM

FORK HILL RD

BULL RUN TRAIL

SEVEN MILE RD

YOUNG WOMANS CREEK RD

DONUT HOLE TRAIL

COUGAR RUN TRAIL

ABES FORK RD

FYE CAMP
TRAIL

LONG FORK
TRAIL

LOG HOLLOW TRAIL

HYNER RUN
STATE PARK

PARKING ★

DRY RUN RD

TO RENOVO

PA 120

HYNER

0
miles
km
0
2
2

on Six Mile Road to 7 miles (11.3 km), where you turn right on a jeep road. At 7.8 miles (12.4 km) turn left onto a trail that descends to Seven Mile Run. At 9.2 miles (14.8 km) cross the run and bear left on Seven Mile Road; along this next stretch you cross a piece of private land. When you reach Young Womans Creek, turn left to cross the stream via the road bridge. Young Womans Creek is a famous trout stream. According to legend the name stems from colonial times when an Indian, fearing approaching pursuers, killed a young woman captive at the creek's mouth. The young woman's ghost then haunted the vicinity, reappearing whenever her killer returned to the creek. On a more positive note, a marker on the right just beyond the bridge commemorates the first purchase of state forest land back in the 1890s.

Back on the trail, turn right in front of Bull Run hunting camp, cross Bull Run, and head upstream on an old grade. The grade soon gives out but the trail keeps mostly to the right of the stream. Plenty of good campsites lie along Bull Run; when you see one you like, set up your home for the night.

Second Day

Bull Run to Ole Bull State Park
Distance: 11.2 miles (18 km)
Walking time: 7 hours
This morning continue up Bull Run and turn left up a side stream at 11.9 miles (19.1 km). You pass a trail regis-ter just before reaching Fork Hill Road. Turn right on the road and follow it to the orange-blazed Susquehannock Trail at 13.6 miles (21.5 km), where Morgan Hollow Trail comes in on your left. Continue on Fork Hill Road to Rattlesnake Trail, where you turn left. Moving along, you pass the blue-blazed Wildcat Trail on your right at 14.9 miles (23.9 km). This is the South Link Trail, which goes east to the Black Forest Trail.

Rattlesnake Trail intersects Hartman Trail at 16.3 miles (26.3 km); bear right along the edge of an impressive log-ging railroad cut to follow Hartman Trail down to Big Spring Branch. You walk along a number of old railroad grades and contemporary roads, so watch the blazes closely as you swing from one side of this valley to the other. At 17.1 miles (27.6 km) you pass the blue-blazed North Link Trail, which also leads east to the Black Forest Trail. Next is a spring house with a stream of cold water, the first good water since Bull Run.

Now move through Spook Hollow, an evergreen plantation, and at the top of the hollow turn left onto a jeep road, and then left again onto Twelve Mile Road at 18.4 miles (29.6 km). After about 200 yards (200 meters) turn right onto Impson Hollow Trail. At 19.5 miles (31.4 km) turn right once more and follow switchbacks up to the plateau again. On the far side you descend to an overlook of Kettle Creek Valley, then move along switchbacks down to PA 144. Once you cross the highway and descend the bank, you're in Ole Bull State Park near your car.

49 R. B. Winter to Poe Paddy

Time allowed: 3 days, 2 nights
Total distance: 24.2 miles (38.9 km)
Walking time: 15 hours
Vertical rise: 3,500 feet (1,070 meters)

An unfortunate feature of this hike across Bald Eagle State Forest is the large amount of oak kill inflicted by the gypsy moth. The gypsy moth suddenly appeared in this area in the early 1970s and, without the deterrence of a natural enemy, began defoliating the oak forests. At several points you see salvage cuts where dead oaks were logged, mostly for pulpwood. In 1978 two species of super fly, introduced to North America in the early 1900s to fight the gypsy moth, followed them into Bald Eagle. The flies are not supposed to bite or sting humans so if a big, black fly the size of the end of your thumb lands on you, don't panic or swat it. It's probably licking the sweat off you and will presently go about its business of destroying gypsy moth caterpillars.

This hike crosses Bald Eagle State Forest on a section of the Mid State Trail, roughly following the eastern boundary of Centre County. The forest is named for an Indian chief whose village was on Bald Eagle Creek in the early 1800s. On this hike, you walk the only foot trail in the commonwealth to pass through a tunnel, the one under Paddy Mountain near the trip's end.

You need a car shuttle. First drive to Poe Valley State Park by following signs from US 322 south of Potters Mills or from PA 45 west of Millheim. Check in at the park office for parking directions at the Poe Paddy picnic area, 3 miles farther east on Big Poe Road. Poe Paddy, a small park oper-

At Horse Path Spring

ated as an overflow area for Poe Valley, is named for its location at the junction of Poe Valley and Paddy Mountain.

Now drive back up Big Poe Road, turn right on the Millheim-Siglerville Turnpike, go to Penns Creek Road, and take the paved road on the right after Neff's Mill. Turn right on PA 45 and drive to the only traffic light in Millheim, turn left onto PA 445, and go through the Millheim Narrows to Brush Valley and PA 192. Turn right onto PA 192 and drive through Livonia to R.B. Winter State Park on the Centre-Union county line. Again, check at the park office for parking information.

First Day

R.B. Winter State Park to Buffalo Creek
Distance: 8.1 miles (13 km)
Walking time: 5 hours

This backpacking trip begins at the PA 192 bridge over Rapid Run at the outlet by the dam. Follow the orange blazes into an evergreen plantation along Rapid Run and then swing right onto Brush Hollow Trail along the park boundary. You cross Yankee Run Trail at 2 miles (3.3 km) and pass a spring to the left. By now it's obvious you're on the grade of an old logging railroad, this one operated by the Laurelton Lumber Company.

Next cross Oley Camp Trail and Douty Mill Trail (there's a stream in the woods off to the right), and approach Stover Gap Road across a large salvage cut. Continue straight ahead on Stover Gap Road, which gently climbs the north side of Shriner Mountain.

At 5.3 miles (8.5 km) turn left into the woods on Hairy Johns Trail, with Horse Path Spring just across the road. You soon cross Fallen Timber Trail. Continue downhill to cross Panther Trail and Panther Run at 5.8 miles (9.4 km). At the edge of Buck Ridge bear left down the south side to cross Pine Creek Road, and continue ahead on Kessler Trail across Pine Creek. Kessler Trail forms the western boundary of the Hook Natural Area (see Hike 27), so if it's late camp here, to the right of the trail, as camping is prohibited in the natural area.

Next climb the steep, north flank of Sharpback Mountain and at 7.6 miles (12.3 km) continue across Negro Hollow Road, named for a black man who ran a logging camp just east of here. The Hook boundary turns east but you continue ahead on Kessler Trail up Buffalo Mountain to Buffalo Creek at 8.1 miles (13 km). This is your first night's camp spot. Higher ground lies on the north side, closer to the creek. Buffalo Creek usually flows all year and despite its weak tea appearance is good for drinking. If the creek is too low, you can reach other water by continuing ahead, down the south flank of Buffalo Mountain, where you should camp at least 200 feet (70 meters) in from Stony Run Road. Water can be obtained at Cinder Pile Spring about 150 yards (150 meters) along the road, to your right.

Second Day

Buffalo Creek to Libby Run
Distance: 10.4 miles (16.8 km)
Walking time: 7 hours

Today you hike farther than on the other two days, but you get off to a good start by descending the south flank of Buffalo Mountain. You then turn right on Stony Run Road at 8.8 miles (14.2 km), pass Cinder Pile Spring, and bear left on the Bucknell Outing Club Trail. Next, rock hop across Sheesley Run and continue to the Sheesley Hollow Trail, turn left, and pass a couple of false summits on the way up Winkelblech Mountain. At the top turn right on the Winkelblech Trail. At 10 miles (16.3 km) turn left on the Hairy Johns Trail for a very steep descent of Winkelblech's south flank; then move to the spring at Hairy Johns Picnic Area on PA 45. Hairy John Vonida was a hermit who lived here along the old stage road after his family died in an epidemic. He brought water to the stagecoach passengers but apparently never spoke with anyone.

After crossing PA 45 make a short climb over Sand Mountain before dropping into Sand Hollow. At 12.4 miles (20 km) you pass the blue-blazed Bear Gap Trail, which goes left to a good campsite, and soon reach Woodward Gap Road and Johnson Spring at 14.6 miles (23.5 km). Bear right on the road to a junction with the Rock Knob Trail, turn left, and start the serious climb up Thick Mountain. About 150 yards (150 meters) be-

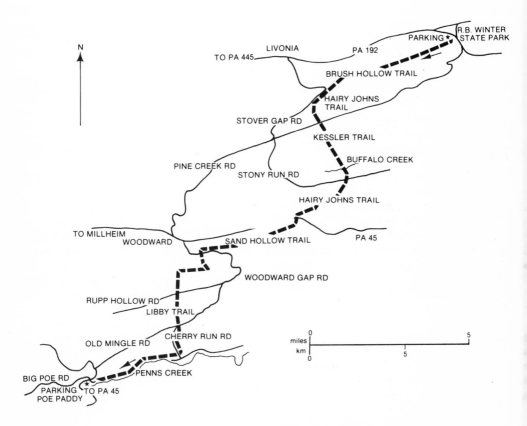

yond the top edge of Thick Mountain drop your pack and follow a short unblazed trail left to the top of Rock Knob. On a clear day you see the tops of several ridges to the south.

Back on the trail you dip slightly to the headwaters of Bear Run, which flows most of the time. At 16 miles (25.7 km) turn right on the Bear Run Trail, follow it to its end, and turn right on the Susquehanna University Outing Club Trail. This trail leads you back to the north edge of Thick Mountain,

where you overlook the east end of Penns Valley. Move across the top of the mountain and bear right on an old wagon road, the Libby Trail. At 17.8 miles (28.7 km) cross Rupp Hollow Road, continue down the Libby Trail to Libby Run and your second night's campsite.

Third Day

Libby Run to Poe Paddy Picnic Area
Distance: 5.7 miles (9.1 km)
Walking time: 3 hours
Your last day on the Mid State Trail

is easy. First, follow Libby Run through its gap between Sawmill Mountain and First Green Knob. Then turn left on the Old Mingle Road for about 300 yards (300 meters) and take a sharp right on Cherry Run Road through a gap in Paddy Mountain. At 20.3 miles (32.7 km) you make your only climb of the day up the steep bank of the old Pennsylvania Railroad and hike upstream along Penns Creek.

Near the end of the hike you pass through a short tunnel under Paddy Mountain and then cross Penns Creek on the old railroad bridge. Turn left on the next road, follow it through one of the sites alleged to be the ghost town of Poes Mills, and come to Poe Paddy and your car. If you've time (and the season is right), stop for a swim at Poe Valley State Park before heading home.

50 Quehanna Trail

Time allowed: 7 days, 6 nights
Total distance: 74.7 miles (119.8 km)
Walking time: 45 hours
Vertical rise: 8,130 feet (2,480 meters)

Tenting on the Quehanna

The Quehanna's wild and beautiful country offers you a real challenge, even if you're an experienced back-packer. For nearly 34 miles (55 km), the trail traverses the Quehanna Wild Area, Pennsylvania's largest such pre-serve, and it also passes through the Marion Brooks Natural Area. Along the way you are likely to see a profusion of wildlife, including fox, beaver, and the particularly abundant deer. The largest bear I have seen outside a zoo was on the Quehanna.

Opened in 1976, the loop trail has not yet attracted the use it merits. In thirteen days of hiking here I met only two other people. Don't try the Que-hanna until you've done a couple of backpacking trips. However, if you wish to try part of the trail, two blue-blazed connectors form shorter loops of about 17 and 50 miles (28 and 79 km).

When I hiked the Quehanna (1977), I encountered problems with blazing. Some turns lacked double blazes and at others I couldn't see the double blaze until after turning. At still others an attempt was made to vary the standard double blaze by displacing the upper blaze in the direction of the turn—but in twenty-five percent of such cases it pointed the wrong way! Also the blazes tended to be too far apart along those sections where new trail had been cut through the woods, although they are well sighted and usually placed on both sides of a tree. Along at least one section the orange paint faded completely away, and I had to follow old ax blazes. Finally, there is the infamous corner 1994, where the orange blazes proceeded in two different directions! I hope by the time you hike, the trail has been re-blazed and these problems corrected. Be sure to obtain a free, detailed map of the trail by writing to Moshannon State Forest, 1229 South Second Street, Box 341, Clearfield, PA 16830, or to Elk State Forest, RD 1, Route 155, Box 327, Emporium, PA 15834.

The trail's backpacking rules pro-hibit camping in the state game lands, Marion Brooks Natural Area, and with-in 100 yards (100 meters) of a drive-able road. You should not camp more than two consecutive nights at any one site, and, according to the trail-head sign at Parker Dam, groups are limited to six persons. You may obtain exception to the person limit by apply-ing to the Moshannon or Elk forest offices in advance. Be extremely care-ful with fire as the area has been devastated by the oak-leaf roller and dead trees abound. A small backpack-ing stove presents a minimal fire hazard.

To reach the trailhead in Parker Dam State Park take Exit 18 off I-80, drive north on PA 153 for 5.1 miles, and bear right on Mud Run Road for 2.6 miles to the park office. Check in, drive back to the campground road and then along it to the large sign-board at the trailhead. If you decide to use a food drop halfway around the loop, the ideal place to spot a car is at the white forestry barn on Wykoff Road 5.2 miles from its intersection with the Quehanna Highway and 4.7

miles from PA 120 at Sinnemahoning. Be sure to notify the Emporium Forestry Office (814-483-3354) if you leave a car there.

First Day

Parker Dam State Park to Roberts Run
Distance: 9.3 miles (15 km)
Walking time: 6 hours

Shoulder your pack and head up the Log Slide Trail. A small part of the slide is reconstructed here. Cross a couple of pipelines, jog right on the CPL Trail, and resume hiking up Little Laurel Run. CPL stands for Central Pennsylvania Lumber Company, which in the early 1900s was the logging subsidiary of the United States Leather Company. At 2.5 miles (4 km) jog left on Laurel Run Road. You soon recross it, cross Tyler Road and an extensive meadow where you are likely to see deer, and finally, at 4.3 miles (7 km), arrive at the junction of McGeorge and Wallace Mine roads. Continue on Wallace Mine Road to a jeep road at 4.8 miles (7.8 km), where you turn right. The short blue-blazed connector trail continues ahead on Wallace Mine Road.

Next, bear left in front of a hunting camp, which has a good spring on the far side, and then move downstream along the Alex Branch. At 5.8 miles (9.4 km) you climb away from it to avoid private land and soon enter State Game Land 94. At 6.7 miles (10.8 km) you reach a pipeline. Drop your pack here and walk ahead about 100 yards (100 meters) on an orange-blazed side trail for a view across Trout Run. Back on the trail, follow the pipeline swath down and across Trout Run to an old railroad grade, turn right, and swing around east into Roberts Run. The grade disappears and you keep to the left of the run and pass among large sandstone boulders. At 8.6 miles (13.8 km) leave the game land and at 9.3 miles (15 km) swing right and cross a boggy meadow on an old beaver dam. Cross Roberts Run as best you can. You can camp on top of the hill on the far side; there's a spring at its base.

Second Day

Roberts Run to Twelve Mile Run
Distance: 14 miles (22.5 km)
Walking time: 8 hours

This is your longest day so get an early start. Follow a series of woods roads and jeep roads to a right turn onto Knobs Road at 11.2 miles (18 km). At 11.7 miles (18.8 km) you turn left and follow more old roads to 12.4 miles (20 km), where you bear right along the state forest boundary. At the corner of state forest land bear left and follow the trail through the woods, paralleling the Caledonia Pike.

Cross the Pike, follow jeep roads down to Gifford Run, cross the run on a bridge and follow the trail downstream on the far side. At 15.4 miles (24.9 km) you cross a side stream (the last water until Twelve Mile Run), and climb to a view across Gifford Run. Watch the blazes carefully as the trail heads through the woods to Merrill

Road. Turn left here on a jeep road and then bear right on a woods road at the border of the Quehanna Wild Area. Next, pass under a large power line, and continue to 18.6 miles (29.9 km) to turn right along the white-blazed border of State Game Land 34. You can't see the double blaze here until after you've turned. Turn right on Lost Run Road at 19 miles (30.6 km); notice the blue-blazed medium-length connector trail that goes left here.

You take Lost Run Road under another power line, then turn left on a woods road at 19.9 miles (32 km), bear right at the road's end, and continue under a large power line. Next pass through a stand of white birch and make a steep descent along a narrow ridge between Gifford Run and Mosquito Creek. At the brink of the final cliffs bear right and then at the base cut left to continue past a hunting camp. You cross Mosquito Creek on a swing bridge at 23.2 miles (37.4 km). Turn right for the short distance to Twelve Mile Run, which, though smaller than Mosquito, is preferable for drinking. Camp back from the stream.

Third Day

Twelve Mile Run to Rider Draft
Distance: 7.4 miles (11.8 km)
Walking time: 4 hours
This is your shortest day, so relax a bit after yesterday's big push and look around at this curious meadow you camped in. Why isn't this valley V-shaped like all the others? Following

the trail a bit farther you see a stone wall bordering the meadow. Just before you turn and climb out of the valley large piles of rocks mark the meadow's downstream end. They are the ruins of Corporation Dam, a splash dam built in the last century that blocked Gifford, Mosquito, and Twelve Mile runs. The meadow formed as the dam filled with sand and silt. Eventually Mosquito Creek cut through the dam and carved a minicanyon through the meadow. Notice the stumps along Mosquito Creek are at the level of the original land surface, considerably below the meadow's.

Your climb out of Mosquito Creek Valley is the first real one on the trail. Just opposite those piles of stones turn sharply left and follow an old wagon road past House Rock at a false summit to the plateau, then proceed along a new trail to 25.2 miles (40.5 km), where you cross under a power line and continue on a woods road. You then follow a series of woods roads to the Cole Run crossing at 28.1 miles (45.3 km) and beyond it pass through several salvage cuts before crossing the Quehanna Highway at 29.3 miles (47.1 km). Beyond the highway continue along the left side of a power line across Marks Run, which drains the Piper Industrial Area so don't drink from it. At the next hilltop turn left onto a grassy logging road through a large salvage cut, descend into Rider Draft, turn right on a jeep road, and reach Rider Spring at 30.6 miles (49.3 km). Camp on the hill above, not near, the hunting camp.

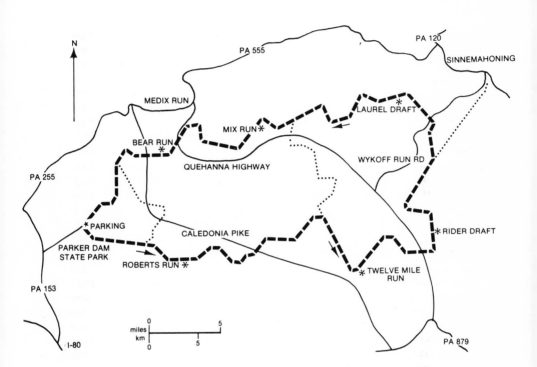

Fourth Day

Rider Draft to Laurel Draft
Distance: 11.5 miles (18.5 km)
Walking time: 7 hours

Your pack should be lighter now. If you've made a food drop at Wykoff Run, it will be a lot lighter. Circle around "Ryders Spring Camp" and make your way up the draw behind it. Soon you bear right, out of the draw, and follow an old fire lane to a small power line at 31.1 miles (50.1 km). From there you move straight across the hill to the end of an old logging road and out to Upper Three Runs

Road and a right turn at 33.4 miles (53.7 km). Follow the road downhill across Upper Three Runs, bear left on the Old Sinnemahoning Road (which has reverted to trail), and climb gently back to the plateau to enter a salvage cut near the top. At the cut's far side bear left, pass through a fringe of woods and turn right on the Three Runs Road. Along this piece of road you cross three blue-blazed cross-country ski trails.

At 35.7 miles (57.5 km) continue ahead on the Old Sinnemahoning Road where the Three Runs Road swings right, and pass another ski trail on the right. At 37.7 miles (60.7 km) pass under a power line and start watching closely for an obscure but vital left turn at 38.1 miles (61.4 km). The orange blazes have faded away so look for ax blazes. A couple of trees lie across the road immediately beyond the turn. You can't see the double blaze until after you've made the turn. (If you miss it you soon come to a pipeline swath.)

After turning left you reach the ruins of an old hunting camp. Continue into the draw to follow it down as best you can. This is Upper Pine Hollow, and it is without much footway. At the bottom you may have to wade across Wykoff Run. Then bear right past the forestry barn. If you have a food drop here your pack gets heavy again, but at least you can leave your trash bag in the car.

Follow the drive out to the Wykoff Road, turn right, and just beyond the bridge turn left up Laurel Draft. This major climb comes at the day's end but the footway is exceptionally good. Camp towards the top of the draft, where the valley widens and before you reach the bridge.

Fifth Day

Laurel Draft to Mix Run
Distance: 12.5 miles (20 km)
Walking time: 8 hours

After starting, you soon cross Laurel Draft, a pipeline and a power line, and then the draft again to go past several beaver dams. At 43.3 miles (69.7 km) you cross Hoover Road, continue down a woods road to a small meadow, bear right and follow a new trail to the end of a jeep road at 44.9 miles (72.2 km). Continue on the jeep road to Corner 1994 at 45.7 miles (73.6 km). At the time I hiked, this was the most confusing spot on the trail. Don't follow the blazed jeep road to the left, but go straight ahead into the woods, following Sanders Draft. Soon you cross over to the left side of the stream and pick up a faint footway. The trail crosses to the other side at several places. At 47.3 miles (76.1 km) the two forks of Sanders Draft come together. From here you have good footway downstream to Red Run. Cross Red Run on rocks. You can avoid the danger of high water by bushwhacking to a road bridge .5 mile (800 meters) downstream.

At 48.1 miles (77.4 km) bear right on Red Run Road. Turn left up Porcupine Draft just before the road bridge over Red Run. You follow an old railroad grade up but the climbing is tough when it gives out. Sometimes you even go right up the stream.

At 50 miles (80.5 km) pick up a dug footway, climb steadily up the side of Porcupine Draft, and go through open woods to a forest road at 50.6 miles (81.4 km). Turn left on the road, right on a pipeline swath, left on Mud Lick Road and shortly right on another road. The blue-blazed medium-length connector trail comes up Losey Road to this junction. At 51.9 miles (83.5 km) you turn left into the Marion Brooks Natural Area and then at 53 miles (85.3 km) left again on a forest road. At the intersection with Deible Road turn sharply right on a jeep road to a hunting camp and continue on a trail down Deible Run. At 54.6 miles (87.8 km) you reach Mix Run and turn upstream. Camp anywhere that looks good.

Sixth Day

Mix Run to Bear Run
Distance: 9 miles (14.4 km)
Walking time: 5 hours

After the last two days this one is easy. Tom Mix, the cowboy star of silent films, was born downstream where Mix Run meets Bennett Branch. Continue upstream along Mix Run. The trail stays to the left side at first but just beyond Camp Hide Out it goes right, back into the brush along the run instead of following the obvious grade up the slope. At 57.6 miles (92.7 km) you turn left between two hunting camps to a junction with a forest road. The Quehanna Highway is visible to your left. Move ahead on the jeep road, turn onto a woods road, and walk to the white-blazed boundary of State Game Land 34 at 59 miles (95 km). Continue down Silver Mill Hollow, reenter state forest land, cross the stream, jog left on a pipeline swath, and reenter the woods on the far side. Soon you pick up a dug footway that slabs the hillside. At 62.1 miles (100 km), after crossing several pipelines and a power line, you cross the Quehanna Highway and Sullivan Run and pick up the dug footway again. Jog right at 62.9 miles (101.3 km) on the Medix grade, cross a swing bridge over Medix Run and turn upstream. At 63.3 miles (102 km) turn right and start the climb up Bear Run. Camp as far up the run as you can before the pipeline swath.

Seventh Day

Bear Run to Parker Dam State Park
Distance: 11 miles (17.6 km)
Walking time: 7 hours

Continue up Bear Run and at 64.3 miles (103.5 km), turn right on a jeep road along a pipeline swath, cross the Caledonia Pike, and continue ahead. At 65.7 miles (105.7 km), partway across a meadow, keep right. Then bear left at successive forks in the road, which begins to descend. Turn left on another jeep road near the bottom of the hill, which goes upstream above Laurel Run. At 67.7 miles (108.9 km), turn left on Saunders Road; just around the bend the short blue-blazed connector trail comes in from the left. Continue to a grassy road just beyond a piped spring on your left at 68.6 miles (110.4 km), and bear right. Continue up and across Big Saunders Run.

After crossing two pipelines, watch for a sharp turn to the right on an old railroad grade. Follow the grade uphill to a right turn onto a jeep road, then continue on a woods road to 71.6 miles (115.2 km) where you turn right towards a clearing visible through the trees. If you follow the woods road across a small meadow you missed this turn. Cross two more pipelines, turn left onto a jeep road, and then cross another pipeline. At 73.2 miles (117.8 km) you cross Tyler Road. Continue on a gated road through Parker Dam State Park, cross a power-line swath, and at 74.2 miles (119.4 km) reenter civilization at the Campground RV dump station. Continue ahead on the paved road to where you began.

Guidebooks from New Hampshire Publishing Company

Written for people of all ages and experience, these highly popular and carefully prepared books feature detailed trail directions, notes on historical and natural points of interest, sketch maps, and photographs.

Fifty Hikes in Connecticut. By Gerry and Sue Hardy $6.95

Fifty Hikes in Massachusetts. By Paul and Ruth Sadlier $6.95

Fifty Hikes in New Hampshire's White Mountains. By Daniel Doan $6.95

Fifty More Hikes in New Hampshire. By Daniel Doan $6.95

Fifty Hikes in Vermont. By Ruth and Paul Sadlier $6.95

Fifty Hikes in Maine. By John Gibson $6.95

Fifty Hikes in Central Pennsylvania. By Tom Thwaites $6.95

In the 25 Walks series—

25 Hikes in the Finger Lakes Region (NY). By Bill Ehling $4.95

25 Walks in Rhode Island. By Ken Weber $4.95

25 Walks in the Dartmouth-Lake Sunapee Region (NH). By Mary L. Kibling $4.95

25 Walks in the Lakes Region (NH). By Paul Blaisdell $4.95

In the *Bike Tours* series—

25 Bike Tours in Vermont. By John Freiden $5.95

25 Bike Tours in New Hampshire. By Thomas and Susan Heavey $5.95

In the *25 Ski Tours* series—

25 Ski Tours in Western Massachusetts. By John Frado, Richard Lawson, and Robert Coy $4.95

25 Ski Tours in Connecticut. By Stan Wass with David Alvord $4.95

25 Ski Tours in the Green Mountains (VT). By Sally and Daniel Ford $4.95

25 Ski Tours in the White Mountains (NH). By Sally and Daniel Ford $4.95

Other outdoor recreation books—

A Year with New England's Birds: A Guide to Twenty-five Field Trips. By Sandy Mallett $5.95

Canoe Camping Vermont and New Hampshire Rivers. By Roioli Schweiker $4.95

Dan Doan's Fitness Program for Hikers and Cross-Country Skiers. By Daniel Doan $4.95

Available from bookstores, sporting goods outlets, or the publisher: New Hampshire Publishing Company, Box 70, Somersworth, NH 03878.